The Long Haul

Books by Robert Carse

Adult

The Age of Piracy
Blockade
Rum Row
The Moonrakers

Juvenile

The Winner
Great Venture
Winter of the Whale
Friends of the Wolf
Turnabout
Glory Haul
Hudson River Hayride
The Young Colonials
Great American Harbors
Go Away Home
Fire in the Night
The Long Haul

THE UNITED STATES MERCHANT

ROBERT CARSE

The
Long Haul

SERVICE IN WORLD WAR II

W·W·Norton & Company·Inc·

New York

In memory of the men and the ships

List of Photographs

ACKNOWLEDGMENTS

Gratitude is expressed here to the people who have been of the utmost assistance to me in the writing of this book. They are: Frank O. Braynard of the Moran Towing and Transportation Company; Lt. Commander Harry A. Hart, USMS, United States Merchant Marine Academy, Kings Point, New York; Vice Admiral Emory S. Land, USN (Ret.), who although an extraordinarily busy man found time to write the introduction; Bart J. McGarry, Public Information Officer, United States Maritime Administration, New York City; and John S. Tennant, Public Information Officer, United States Maritime Administration, Washington, D.C.

Photographs pages 32-33 and 40-41 courtesy the Imperial War Museum, London; all other photographs courtesy the U.S. Maritime Administration.

INTRODUCTION

The record of World War II shows that 5,638 men of the United States Merchant Marine gave their lives to keep the ships sailing. This loss was from a total of a quarter of a million men involved. But in the vital year of 1942-43, the maximum number of men in the service was not more than 100,000, and all of them were volunteers.

A great deal might be said by me about the fashion in which they served and how the ships they took to sea were built. It is perhaps enough to say that without the "long haul" of the ships, the slow, steady, and unbroken movement of troops and cargoes around the world, the war would not have been won.

Dwight D. Eisenhower, General of the Army and Supreme Commander of the Allied Expeditionary Forces, wrote from his headquarters at London in 1944 a statement that sums up the account quite well. He said that the men of the United States Merchant Marine served with "a devotion to duty and a disregard for danger and hardship that defies any attempt to describe."

Emory S. Land,
Vice Admiral, USN (Ret.)
U.S. War Shipping Administrator,
World War II

WHERE MANY SHIPS PASS. The United States Merchant Marine Memorial Chapel looks out toward the East River and the Port of New York. It is a national monument erected on the grounds of the Merchant Marine Academy at Kings Point, New York, as tribute to the men of the service who lost their lives in wartime.

THE men knew. The crews that took the American merchant marine ships to sea understood as early as 1939 that the nation would certainly be involved in war with Germany, and very probably also with Italy and Japan. For the old-timers in the ships, the shape of the future was unmistakable. They recalled the years between 1914 and 1917, when Great Britain and France gradually drew in the United States as a full ally.

This would be repeated, the old-timers said, once Hitler's Germany started to attack. The younger men in the crews carefully listened. They had already seen enough evidence of oncoming war in the ports around the world where their ships called.

A considerable part of the crews, too, belonged to the National Maritime Union. About eight hundred men from it had volunteered to fight in the Spanish Republican Army in the 1936-1939 civil war, and two hundred of them were killed. There in Spain, the NMU members said during the forecastle talks at sea, the new, the second, world war had begun. And it was too late now to stop that. The war could only spread.

There was rarely any argument left at the end of the shipboard talks. Men from American merchant ships had stood on Hamburg street corners in the middle 1930's and handed out anti-Nazi pamphlets and made speeches against Hitler. They had been badly beaten as a result, and a couple of them were sent to prison by Hitler's judges. So when the big North German Lloyd passenger liner *Bremen* came into the Port of New York, a picked group of American seamen visited her.

They slipped aft to the fantail, and while two of them worked out their dislike of Hitler upon some of the crew, the third volunteer tore the swastika ensign from the stern pole and threw it into the Hudson River. Police were called to intervene, finally, but the ensign was not recovered, and the Americans engaged in the incident were released.

This became a classic example of defiance of the enemy. American merchant seamen stood on the Bund in Shanghai and protested the Japanese occupation of China. They wrestled with Mussolini's black-shirted *squadristi* in Naples and Genoa and vehemently criticized the Italian seizure of Ethiopia. They raised contributions for political refugees, smuggled anti-Nazi and anti-Fascist literature into Germany and Italy, and recklessly risked their lives.

Not all members of ships' crews joined in the action Most of the men who participated were regarded by their shipmates as "screwballs" or part of the "Commie fringe." But the main facts were agreed upon, and when the Pearl Harbor attack came on December 7, 1941, nearly all of the merchant seamen, both unlicensed personnel and officers, decided to stay with the ships.

Six American ships had already been sunk during the strange war-no-war period that led to the Pearl Harbor attack. The first of them to take a U-boat torpedo was the *Robin Moor*, a freighter with the stars and stripes painted broadly on her sides to identify her as a neutral. She was hit on May 21, 1941, while more than halfway across the Atlantic and bound for African ports. Her crew got safely off her in three boats and, when they were brought back Stateside, soon shipped out again.

Pearl Harbor did not have any particular effect upon them or the rest of the 85,000 men in the merchant marine. They had anticipated it for too long, and since President Roosevelt's declaration of national emergency in May, 1941, they had recognized that what they met at sea was war. United States Navy ships served as escorts for the merchant vessels that ran the North Atlantic. Troops and supplies were being sent to Iceland to relieve the British garrison there. No attempt was made to disguise the deckloads of tanks, planes, trucks, and drums of high-octane gas aboard the ships that sailed during the fall months of 1941 from East Coast ports. A "shoot on sight" order had been issued by the President after the destroyer U.S.S. *Greer* was attacked by a U-boat.

Pearl Harbor, the merchant seamen said, just brought in

the Japs. But they admitted that it greatly extended the war. Then, despite all of their previous knowledge, they began to realize the frightful strain that was being put upon them. It was almost incalculable. They were still less than 100,000 men, even with those who could be mustered from the beach. There were three hundred ships in commission for them to sail, most of the freighters at least twenty years old. With that fleet, they had to haul troops, munitions, and supplies to every continent along a vast complex of sea routes that reached to Reykjavík and Archangel, and to Port Moresby, to Capetown and the Persian Gulf, and around Cape Horn.

The Atlantic Ocean was at the center of the complex, and for the Allies an absolutely vital area. It had to be traversed by great and constantly moving masses of shipping or the United States' three principal allies, Britain, the Soviet Union, and China, would not be able to continue the war. The western fronts in Europe, the Mediterranean front, the Russian front, and even the land front in Asia were all heavily supplied by the Atlantic routes.

Hitler knew this very well. He gave command of the German sea attack to a skillful, ruthless veteran, Admiral Karl Doenitz, who had served in U-boats in World War I and was extremely efficient in his planning of the blockade of Great Britain. The Nazis hoped that they could starve the British out of the war.

Doenitz worked to girdle the British Isles with mine fields, aircraft patrols, and U-boat zones of operation, while he sent his surface raiders and a number of his bigger U-boats ranging thousands of miles from their home bases. German air attacks were concentrated on Britain. Without doubt, the British Isles would be the site from which the

Allies would finally mount their counterattack against Germany. The Germans could stop it only from the sea.

When France fell in June, 1940, Doenitz was given a tremendous advantage. He set up his U-boat bases in steel-ribbed, concrete pens in the French Atlantic ports of Lorient, Brest, and Saint-Nazaire, and took for his headquarters a villa at Kernevel, near Lorient on the Bay of Biscay.

The Japanese had not told their German allies that they would attack at Pearl Harbor. So Doenitz and his staff were forced to work with great speed to prepare for sea warfare against the United States. It took them a month to organize what they called Operation *Paukenschlag*. Twenty U-boats were gathered and sent to North American coastal waters and were assigned to stations from Halifax on down to Miami. Their officers and crews were veterans; they had served around the British Isles, in the Mediterranean, and in the Arctic. Doenitz expected that with this flotilla he could sink so many vessels that the American public would be stunned, and as a result the United States war effort, instead of gaining momentum, would falter.

The U-boats were of the type known as VII C. They were 220 feet over-all, and displaced 770 tons. Their speed on the surface was seventeen knots; when submerged they were capable of eight knots. The early models were equipped with four bow torpedo tubes and a single stern tube. Their armament consisted of either twelve or fourteen one-ton torpedoes, a twenty-millimeter antiaircraft gun and a pair of twin machine guns on deck. They could cruise 8,500 miles from base, and carried a crew of forty-four officers and men.

The ships they attacked on January 12, 1942, were for

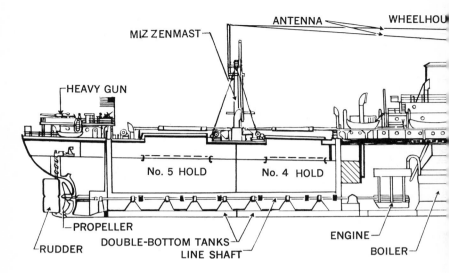

ANTENNA
WHEELHOU
MIZZENMAST
HEAVY GUN
No. 5 HOLD
No. 4 HOLD
PROPELLER
RUDDER
DOUBLE-BOTTOM TANKS
LINE SHAFT
ENGINE
BOILER

the most part freighters whose maximum speed was no greater than that the U-boats maintained when submerged. The American vessels went unarmed and nearly all of them without escort. Escort, when it was available, was made up of wooden-hulled submarine chasers built for World War I service, and half the size of the German underwater craft that waited for them.

Paukenschlag means a stroke upon a kettledrum. This was transmitted as the attack signal by radio from Doenitz's villa, and the twenty U-boats moved closer to the shore to make sure of their targets. The Germans had already sunk 1,017 ships in the war and lost 60 of their own craft. There was a great deal of confidence among the North American flotilla crews. It would be very hard for them to miss an eight-knot ship, unbothered by depth charges, enemy aircraft, or mine fields.

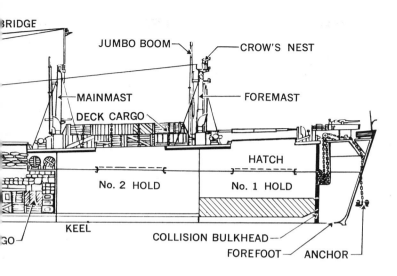

BRIDGE

JUMBO BOOM

CROW'S NEST

MAINMAST

FOREMAST

DECK CARGO

HATCH

No. 2 HOLD

No. 1 HOLD

KEEL

COLLISION BULKHEAD

FOREFOOT

ANCHOR

Ship after ship was sunk as *Paukenschlag* was executed. The German toll of shipping before it began was almost five million tons. The sinkings made here would soon add substantially to that. Doenitz had promised that in March the flotilla would be reinforced by the 1,000-ton tanker submarines. They would supply it with fuel and torpedoes, and the U-boats could stay on the American coast until Doenitz was satisfied with the number of sinkings.

The men in the American ships took the punishment, although it was almost unbearable in its intensity. Escort and air surveillance were practically worthless. Pilots of the Air Patrol were so innocent that they announced over the 600-meter radio band not only its plane routes, but the time schedules.

Many of the U-boat officers had served in the merchant marine, could speak English, and had sailed these waters before. The U-boats also received detailed radio information from spies ashore. Ship movements were relayed to them, times of departure, and estimated times of arrival. The German craft lay on the surface off Miami at night to recharge their batteries while the glare of the hotel lights gleamed upon the lenses of the binoculars used by the watch officers who stood in the conning towers.

All of the men in the American ships—masters, mates, engineers, and unlicensed personnel—were volunteers. None of them was forced to stay aboard ship. There is record of very few who went ashore and took draft-free jobs in shipyards or other essential war industries. The great majority were quite willing to accept the challenge offered them by the Germans and the Japanese. And during the first months of 1942, they were slaughtered.

The men were loners, individualists who had come to the merchant marine and the sea because they disliked life ashore. They had almost equal dislike for the regulations of the United States Navy. It was their proudest boast that they could perform any shipboard task as well as a Navy man in half the time, and with half the labor.

They were, in that cruel, desperate year of 1942, caught up in learning Navy convoy procedure, signaling, and gunnery, and while they were at sea, they were always under Navy orders. If any of them recognized the fact that they served with the same spirit that had been shown in the early American ships, the privateers of the Revolution and the War of 1812, and the blockade vessels of the Civil War, very little was said about it.

The present, just keeping alive, was enough. There was no time to contemplate the past.

THE first ships to be sunk were British, Latvian, and Norwegian, caught by torpedoes with severe loss of life off Halifax and near Long Island and Cape Hatteras. Then the American tanker *Allan Jackson*, bound for New York from Cartagena, was struck. She was bringing in a 72,870-barrel cargo of crude oil and making ten knots over a calm sea. It was one thirty in the morning of January 18, and very dark. The bridge watch stared ahead, looking for Winter Quarter Lightship that marked Diamond Shoals.

Two torpedoes hit *Allan Jackson*, and she was set afire. Men burned to death as they tried to run along her catwalk to the afterhouse and the lifeboat being launched by the bosun and some of the sailors. Captain Felix W. Kretch-mer, the master, was flung into the sea, where for three hundred yards oil blazed around the ship.

The captain was sucked under when the ship sank, but managed to find a piece of debris. He clung to it for seven hours until rescued by a destroyer. Most of his crew were not so lucky. The torpedo blasts smashed them; they were cremated on deck or within the huge, high-blazing pool of oil overside; sharks cruising the Gulf Stream waters found others as they struggled clear.

The terrible pattern that was to be repeated along the Atlantic Coast hundreds of times during the next year had been established. The ships went fast, some in the space of a couple of minutes, and many ablaze. Survivors bore ghastly burns when they reached the beach or were picked up by naval craft. Men talked of wrenching great foul gobs of coagulated oil out of their mouths so that they might breathe and swim. They arrived ashore slick with oil from head to foot, stinking of it, eyes, ears, and mouths crusted.

When they stopped shaking and could speak coherently, they told of U-boat crews that trained searchlight beams upon them in the water, took photographs, and laughed at the calls for help. It became increasingly common for the U-boats to save their torpedoes, sinking the vessels by gunfire. Chases went on for hours; when Captain John Dodge of the tanker *Malay* brought his badly battered ship to final safety inside Old Point Comfort, Virginia, *Malay* had been pounded by gunfire, then hit amidships by a torpedo during a two-hour chase.

Twenty ships were sunk by the U-boats, and two hundred merchant seamen killed in the first two weeks of

LIBERTY AND LADY. A heavily laden Liberty ship waits at the anchor for convoy orders, the Statue of Liberty behind her in Upper New York Bay. This was one of the ships that managed to deliver an average of 6,000 long tons of cargo an hour during the course of the war.

the operation. A vast and curious, oil-drenched litter appeared on American beaches from Maine to Miami. Sightseers made a habit of examining it, occasionally turning up part of an incinerated body. But nothing was done to dim the brilliance of the coastal resort lights as requested by the Navy and the sea unions. The hotel owners and the people who ran night clubs and restaurants in the port cities were reluctant to obey blackout regulations. They wanted to attract customers, they said, and not scare them away. If their lights set the ships alongshore in clear silhouette for the U-boats, they were sorry.

Some of the men who survived a coastal run in the worst months of 1942 were unable to go back to sea. Their nerves made return impossible for them. When ashore, they shivered at the slightest sound, and when a truck backfired in the street outside, they started for the nearest doorway—to abandon ship. They told of seventeen tankers, all ablaze, lying between Five Fathoms Lightship at the mouth of the Delaware River and Navesink, New Jersey. One man who made his way back to New York had been torpedoed twice in the same day; the rescue vessel had been struck soon after he boarded her. "Twice," the survivor said. "Twice inside twenty-four hours. That's too lousy much."

No psychiatric treatment was available for these men. Their problem was not yet recognized by the government or by the public, and they were not even permitted to enter or use servicemen's clubs. Sympathy came only from their shipmates, their families and the members of their unions. But, often, when their nervous condition was extreme and they twitched, jumped, and stuttered, they were resented in the union halls. Men ready to ship out did not like to consider what within a few hours might happen to them.

The torpedoed men took to the bottle. With their pay, alone, clinging to very thin strands of sanity, they registered in hotels in the port cities. Then they bought great quantities of liquor, locked themselves in their rooms, and drank until memory was blank and they lay in stupor. They emerged weak and haggard days later, and still unfit to return to sea.

But pressure was gradually applied by the sea unions, and indignation was expressed in the newspapers and by the public. The Navy protested that it was doing all in its power to reduce the rate of destruction by U-boat. Admiral Adolphus Andrews was placed in command of the Coastal Frontier Forces. He was the Navy's finest antisubmarine officer, and he created immediately a new organization known as Eastern Sea Frontier. It was charged with the safety of all Allied merchant shipping between Canada and Florida.

Navy estimates had put the present U-boat force at thirty vessels operating in Atlantic coastal waters. Admiral Andrews could bring against them only a system of defense created in 1929 and never improved. He had as his entire striking force ten World War I subchasers of wooden construction and three deepwater yachts that had been donated by their owners. This force was supported by six Army bombers and four blimps. None of the units was able to sight the enemy or engage it.

Hitler went on the air in February and in a characteristic screaming, ranting broadcast boasted that the destruction of American merchant shipping was to become much worse. He warned the seamen to leave the ships, said they were fools to go out against the greatly increased U-boat force he had sent into the Atlantic.

Most of the American merchant seamen ashore at the time of the Hitler speech gathered in bars to hear him. Their response was simple, profane, and unprintable. But they could not forget the fact that the U-boat sinkings had reached the rate of two ships a day. Reports from survivors and from Navy sources described a new type of U-boat recently put into operation off the coast. This was a 2,000-ton vessel painted a light gray, with what appeared to be a four-inch deck gun forward of the conning tower and a somewhat smaller piece on the afterdeck.

The protection given by the United States Navy was still negligible, although Navy communiqués said, "Strong countermeasures are being taken by units of the Navy's East Coastal Command." The Navy lacked all types of antisubmarine vessels and aircraft. The Atlantic coast was not considered a high-priority theater of operations.

Transatlantic convoys bound for the United Kingdom, Iceland, and the Soviet Union were given every available naval vessel for escort. Deck guns were put aboard the merchant marine ships assigned to these routes, and so were Navy Armed Guard crews as soon as the men could be trained. The Royal Air Force refused to release a number of American-built bombers that were ready to be flown to the United Kingdom under the lend-lease arrangement. So the Atlantic-coast slaughter continued unchecked.

The U-boat crews in the big new vessels were delighted by the ease with which they were allowed to find their targets. There were so many of them now along the coast that they were forced to show navigational lights at night to keep out of one another's way. Captains exchanged visits, and counted up their sinkings, and calculated when they would have enough for the Iron Cross, and then the Oak Leaves added to that, and a long leave home. Motion-picture films of stricken ships and survivors in lifeboats or in the sea were taken for the record. Machine guns were trained on the men in the lifeboats, and they were reviled and threatened from the U-boat decks; the Germans wanted to get dramatic expression in their pictures.

February was a frightful month for the American merchant seamen, and March was to be worse. But on February 2 the tanker W. L. *Steed*, built in 1918 for the Standard Oil Company of New Jersey, was caught by a pair of U-boats, and the men who survived her destruction went through some of the most extreme suffering of the entire war.

She was bucking a northwesterly snow gale off the Delaware Capes, low in the water with a cargo of 65,000 barrels of oil, and making only eight knots headway. The bridge watch could barely see over the side when at 12:45 A.M. she was struck by a torpedo. It penetrated the hull on the starboard side and exploded in Number Three tank, forward of the bridge, and instantly set the ship afire. The crew were alert because of submarine warnings for several days past, and Captain Harold G. McAvenia, a World War I veteran, had the lifeboats swung out ready in the davits.

He stopped the ship's main engine, told the engine-room force to abandon stations and instructed the second mate, Sydney Wayland, to clear the two midships lifeboats. The general-alarm bell was jangling when Wayland obeyed, and men were already on their way to the boats. All of them

wore life jackets, but a number of them lacked warm clothing, because they came directly from the forecastle or the
messroom.

Mr. Wayland took away fourteen men in Number Two
boat and reported after his rescue that all boats left the
ship. He never saw any of those again, though, and one by
one, the men in his boat died. There were alive at the end
only Einar A. Nilsson, the chief mate, and Wayland. The
chief officer was extremely fatigued and showed signs of
weakness, and Wayland was afraid for his life. Then, about
9:30 A.M. on February 6, a steamer was sighted, and the
boat was seen by her.

She was the British ship *Hartlepool*, bound for Halifax.
She put the two Americans ashore there February 9, and
they were sent to the hospital. Mr. Nilsson died the next
day. When Mr. Wayland recovered from the effects of
what he had suffered, he was returned to the United States.

Number Three boat when she left *Steed* was in command of the bosun, Joaquin Brea. He had with him Able
Seamen Ralph Mazzucco, Raymond Burkholder, and Louis
Hartz, and Ordinary Seaman Arthur Chandler. The high
and very rough seas swung the boat under the stern of the
sinking, blazing tanker which was being swept fore and aft
by shells from the German deck guns. The men crouched
down against the thwarts and stared amazed at the enemy.
Mazzucco later wrote a graphic account of what happened.

The U-boat crews were practicing gunnery despite the
weather conditions and the poor visibility. Soaked, plas-
tered with snow, and secured by life lines, their caps
jammed low, the gunners served the pieces in complete
obedience to the orders given from the conning tower. But

CONVOY. Spread over miles of ocean and protected by cruisers, destroyers, and carrier-borne planes, the tremendous armada proceeds across the Atlantic for the assault upon the French possessions in North Africa. The photo was taken November 26, 1942, while the convoy, composed of transports, tankers, ammunition, and supply ships, moved in perfect formation.

the *Steed* survivors were not given much time to watch that.

A huge cross sea had just carried away all of their oars except three and had taken the tiller, the rudder, the sails, and the boat hooks. The bosun yelled that the boat must be bailed at once or the men would drown. They were numb, flailed by wind, spindrift and snow, and yet in a couple of hours they bailed the boat and were able to rig the canvas cover to give themselves some protection from the storm.

The men talked during the night. They tried to joke and laugh, forget their fear. But Chandler, the ordinary seaman, lay down in the bottom of the boat, and whether he knew it or not, he was seeking death. Mazzucco tried to wake him in the morning and found him dead. The body was carried to the fore part of the boat, in a form of funeral. Then Burkholder became delirious during the same morning and died soon after noon. His body was carried forward.

The men who remained came to the realization that they must get dry and warm or die. A kerosene lamp that was part of the boat's equipment had been broken by the heavy sea. But the kerosene was still in it; there was a hatchet and a water bucket. The boat was made of wood; that would burn.

First, the thwarts were chopped into kindling. Then the stern seats, and the forward seats, and the bottom board, and one of the three oars. The men dried their clothing. They kept the fire going in the water bucket through the rest of the day and into the night. Then they were sighted and picked up by H.M.C.S. *Alcantara*, a Canadian auxiliary cruiser.

The survivors, Brea, who as bosun had been in command

of the boat, and Mazzucco and Hartz were put ashore in Halifax. They suffered severely from frostbite, exposure, and shock. They were duly discharged from the hospital and returned to the United States and went back to sea.

A British ship, *Raby Castle*, sent a report from Capetown, South Africa, that supplied the remaining facts about the tragedy. She had picked up on February 12 a boat that belonged to *W. L. Steed*. Her position at the time was more than four hundred miles east of where the tanker had been sunk. There were four men in the boat; only one of them was alive. He was Elmer E. Maihiot, Jr., who had served aboard *Steed* as second assistant engineer. He was given great care by his rescuers, but he had suffered too much. He died three days after he was picked up, without regaining consciousness.

News of the sinking of *W. L. Steed* was kept from the public. The U-boat onslaught, as Hitler had promised, was increasing daily, and in Feburary and March it was a question of obtaining not only men for the ships but ships themselves. The Allies were very close to defeat in the Atlantic battle. Operation *Paukenschlag* was sinking more vessels than could be built.

There was very little guesswork needed, though, for the shoreside residents in Florida, Delaware, New Jersey, and New York to tell how the war was going. Day and night they heard the U-boat gunfire or the heavy, rumbling slam of a torpedo explosion. Then there was the vast black column of smoke across the seaward sky, laced with flame and rising from the inferno of the ship. The spectacle at night was marked by the abrupt flare of cherry-colored light that meant ignited high-test gasoline or bunker fuel. People lifted their window shades in defiance of blackout regula-

NEAR MISS. Convoy PQ-16, on the way to North Russia in May, 1942, receives heavy enemy attack. A German 1,100 pound aerial bomb is exploded in the sea close to

tions, then dressed and went down to the beach. Sometimes, there were just bodies for the Coast Guard to gather, and occasionally, if the tide was wrong or the wind from the shore, there was nothing, not even a cry.

The *Paukenschlag* toll reached its highest point in the middle of March. Twenty ships were sunk along the Atlantic coast in that week. During little more than two months of U-boat operation, 145 ships had been lost. Their total sum was 800,000 tons; and 600 men from their crews were gone.

Seamen in the waterfront bars looked ruefully at the big posters that told them, "A slip of the lip may sink a ship," and, "Don't blab—the enemy is listening." They could not laugh; the situation was much too serious. But they could curse, and they did. They were very much aware that they

the escort commander's ship, HMS *Ashanti*. Another of
the escort vessels, HMS *Eskimo*, is in the foreground.
Behind them are the slow-moving cargo ships.

were surrounded by spies who collected information every-
where, and only a very little of it came from blabbing heard
in bars. Many of the longshoremen who loaded the ships in
New York harbor were known to be Nazi Party members.
A taxi ride along Twelfth Avenue told a lot, too, and a ride
on the Staten Island ferry. Over on Staten Island, a spy
who worked as a waiter in sailor joints near the docks had
been caught. He had also rented a room up on the heights
over the harbor; he had used powerful binoculars to inspect
the ships that set out to sea, and in the room was a short-
wave radio sending set. Almost every night, when he had
his reports ready, he had been in touch with the *Paukenschlag* operators offshore.

"Give us guns," the seamen said, not caring whether the
spies heard. "This here's become the frantic Atlantic. It's

worse than the terrific Pacific."

During the last day of March, the Navy reported six ships lost through U-boat action. They were *Tiger, T.C. McCobb, Menominee, Allegheny, Barnegat,* and *City of New York.* Passengers were carried by *City of New York,* a motor ship. Among them were three women, and one of those had with her, in her arms, her three-year-old daughter.

Twenty people were in the only lifeboat that was able to get clear of *City of New York* before the ship sank. The vessel went down in a gale while a hundred miles off the coast. There were extreme weather conditions, and within the next ten days half of the men in the boat died of exposure.

It was necessary to get the corpses out of the boat for reasons both of sanitation and morale. But there were no weights to drag them below the surface. When thrust over the side, they very slowly floated away, grotesquely bobbing. The child had cried ever since the ship had been abandoned. With the death of her mother, she gave way to complete hysteria. She asked, "Please don't throw my Mummy in the water. Please don't." Still, her mother was sent to the sea, and thirteen days later the child and the other survivors were brought ashore by a rescue ship.

There were other similar instances along the coast. One little blonde-headed girl was in a lifeboat in winter conditions for thirty-seven hours before being saved. Caught by the prevailing westerly winds, survivors drifted out into the immense wastes of the Atlantic, far from the coastal sea lanes, and usually died of exposure, thirst, and hunger. Only the very lucky were picked up soon after they abandoned ship.

It was not until the middle of May that the first convoys sailed along the coast with Navy escort. They ran between Hampton Roads and Key West; and northward, where there had been so many night sinkings, the "leapfrog" system of daylight navigation was put into effect. Ships coming from Maine anchored overnight in Boston, then used the Cape Cod Canal and Long Island Sound to keep away from the U-boats, and anchored again overnight in New York. There were no such ports available south of Cape Hatteras, so huge ship pens were built.

These were constructed of miles of booms and nets surrounded by mine fields. They were 125 miles apart, and at dusk the ships entered them with their escorts. The Navy had finally taken destroyers from convoy duty on the run to Iceland and assigned them to the Eastern Sea Frontier. The lanky craft, known as "four-pipers" because of their tall, narrow stacks, had been built in 1918, and were rusty and seaworn when they joined the coastal convoys. But they carried five-inch cannon, depth charges, torpedoes, and radar, and to the crews of the merchant ships they were a most welcome sight.

Doenitz, though, was absolutely determined to wreck American shipping on the coast. The toll during the spring of 1942 remained at a daily average of more than two ships sunk. Navy headquarters charts showed the positions of hundreds of lost ships, strewn where they had been last reported along the curve of the continental shelf. Then Doenitz sent his U-boats into the Gulf of Mexico and the Caribbean. These waters were used constantly by a great many Allied ships, and they lacked protection of any sort.

The slaughter became worse than ever, and it was estimated in Washington and London that unless conditions at sea greatly improved, Hitler could enforce his own surrender terms before the end of 1942. An extremely candid correspondence was held between Churchill and Roosevelt as the ship-loss figures mounted, and both men realized that defeat was very close. Even before the U-boat attacks began in the Gulf of Mexico and the Caribbean, a letter written by Roosevelt, on March 18, to Churchill acknowledged the danger. He said in part:

"My Navy has been definitely slack in preparing for this submarine war off our coast. As I need not tell you, most naval officers have declined in the past to think in terms of any vessel of less than two thousand tons. You learned the lesson two years ago. We still have to learn it."

Roosevelt was expressing here the acute need for escort vessels. But the number of merchant marine ships still available had become much too small for a successful continuation of the war. And crews for them were being rapidly exhausted, incapacitated or killed. There was as yet no effective system of replacement for either ships or men.

This was the tremendous problem of the Battle of the Atlantic. It all but obscured the severity of the Pacific sea war, and the keen need in that area for the same kind of replacements. The Pacific routes were much more widely scattered than those in the Atlantic, the ports far apart and mainly in the hands of the enemy.

Japanese submarines and surface craft were manned by alert, active crews who were almost unbelievably cruel in their treatment of prisoners. American merchant seamen in the Pacific theater found themselves just as expendable as

TOUGH ENOUGH. A Liberty ship that survived the full force of a German U-boat torpedo. While her hull is badly ripped and the Number Two Hold gapes wide to the sea, the ship is still under her own power and has reached port.

the American and Filipino soldiers on Bataan. When they were captured, they shared the same miserable existence in the prison camps.

chapter **3**

THE Japanese were much more frank than their Nazi allies about the treatment to be given prisoners. The Imperial Naval Order to the Commander of Submarines, issued right after Pearl Harbor, was blunt:

> "Do not stop with the sinking of enemy ships and cargoes; at the same time you will carry out the complete destruction of the crews of the enemy's ships; if possible seize part of the crew and endeavor to secure information about the enemy."

That meant torture for the American merchant seamen, and they did everything in their power to stay free of the Japanese. But there were long-range Japanese submarines and surface raiders at sea days before the Pearl Harbor attack, and on the day itself the small freighter *Cynthia Olson* was sunk, disappearing with all hands while headed for Honolulu from Puget Sound. Her distress call was heard by the radio operator of the liner *Lurline*, moving at flank speed from Honolulu on her course for San Francisco.

It became Navy theory later that some at least of the *Olson*'s thirty-five people had been taken aboard the Japanese submarine for questioning. Similar tactics were used with other captured crews. But three days after the distress call had been received from the freighter, planes from the U.S.S. *Enterprise* claimed they had sunk a submarine in the area where the message had originated. Americans might well have died under their own countrymen's bombs.

In all parts of the Pacific, ships flying the American flag tried elusive tactics to get home. Captain Orel Arthur Pierson, in command of the liner *President Harding*, tried to make a run on December 7 out of the Yangtze River, below Shanghai, and head past the main Japanese islands for Vladivostok. A patrol plane brought a Japanese cruiser and an armed liner, and *President Harding* was trapped. The best Captain Pierson could do was put her aground at flank speed and tear the bottom plates out of her. He and all of his crew were captured and sent to the dreaded coal mines at Hokkaido.

Far away to the south and beyond Pitcairn Island, the freighter *Vincent*, under Captain Angus Mackinnon, was captured the next day by the armed raiders *Hokoku Maru* and *Aikoku Maru*. Then the freighter *Malama*, commanded by Captain Malcolm Peters, was captured by the same pair. The men in these crews were transferred from

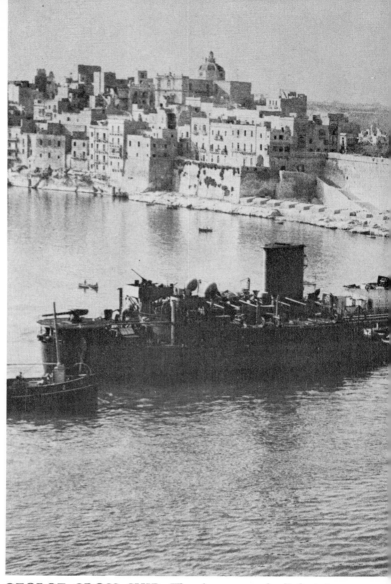

GEORGE CROSS SHIP. The famous and all but indestructible tanker *Ohio* enters Valleta harbor, Malta, on August 22, 1942, in a crippled condition. She has just run the combined German-Italian gantlet of planes, torpedo

boats and submarines, and carries safely a full cargo of gasoline for the R.A.F. squadrons busy in the defense of the island.

one vile prison camp to another for the duration of the war, and many of them died because of the treatment they received.

Japanese submarines were active in the Hawaiian Islands area, and the freighter *Lahaina* was sunk there December 10 after a warning shot from a deck gun had been fired across her bow. She was set afire by deck-gun salvos, and Captain Hans O. Matthieson abandoned with all hands in the one lifeboat that could be used. The submarine crew threatened them with machine-gun fire, but then the craft pulled off and left them. According to Captain Matthieson the Japanese had probably heard patrol-plane motors and were afraid of aerial attack. But the men from *Lahaina* were almost ten days in the boat before she was brought through the surf at Maui, and during the voyage four of them died from exposure to the tropic sun, lack of food, and the drinking of sea water.

Then the freighter *Manini* was sunk in the southwest Pacific by torpedo attack, and after her the *Prusa* and the tanker *Emido* by torpedo and shellfire. The *Emido* was sunk two hundred miles northwest of San Francisco, off Blunt's Reef. The freighters *Exhibitor* and *Exmoor* were attacked thousands of miles away, trying to get home from Calcutta.

They lay at anchor side by side in the Hooghly River before they were given orders on the last of March to sail. Both were loaded with return cargo, but *Exhibitor* had powerful new engines and could turn up a speed of seventeen knots. She was to wait a day and then run by herself while *Exmoor* joined six other ships in a British convoy. Maximum speed for the convoy was estimated at ten knots, and Captain Elbert Wilson, the master of *Exhibitor*, considered himself lucky to have the chance to proceed alone.

She left her Hooghly anchorage at midnight on April 1, 1942, and moved down the river. Her cargo was chrome ore, a vital need in American steel mills, and in Number Six hold she carried several hundred tons of select India tea packed in hundred-pound chests. There was no Royal Air Force cover for the ship as Captain Wilson took her toward the Bay of Bengal. But he was not worried. Units of the Japanese fleet had not yet been reported in the Indian Ocean, and he had been promised fighter-plane escort when he reached the Western Channel Lightship at the mouth of the river after forty-four hours of estimated steaming time.

Exhibitor was nearly out of the river by noon on April 3 when the huge Japanese flying boat, a Kamanishi bearing the red-sun wing markings and the numerals 0-52, attacked from high overhead. It came ripping down the heat-glazed sky; most of those aboard the ship had never seen such a plane before and had difficulty in making the identification. But *Exhibitor* was armed, one of the few American vessels that had been given a four-inch gun aft on the poop and four .50-caliber Browning machine guns in steel-bulwarked tubs at the corners of the main house.

Captain Wilson made out the markings and the numerals through his binoculars while the aircraft circled, climbed, and came back, right on course. Then he saw the bomb slanting downward at the ship, and he leaped from the bridge into the wheelhouse, and grasped and pulled the red handle of the general-alarm bell.

Exhibitor had a company of fifty-eight men, twelve of whom formed the Navy gun crew. While the bomb was still in the air, they started for their battle stations. The Japanese bombardier for some reason chose to release from considerable height, and the bomb was a near-miss, striking the water twenty yards off the port quarter.

The explosion heavily jarred the ship's stern and rudder. She was in a narrow stretch of the river called the Gut, with flat land on both sides and no room to maneuver. Captain Wilson could only hold her ahead, downstream, while the Kamanishi whipped around for another run.

Lief Johan Christiansen was the chief mate aboard Exhibitor. He had been without sleep for two days while he finished the loading in Calcutta and stood anchor watch in the river. Now he was at his station in the gun tub on the port side of the bridge. He threw the safety off the Browning, saw that the belt led correctly, and squinted upward at 0-52, about to make a new run.

The plane passed low overhead this time, and the thrash of the four motors deafened the men below; the propeller suction yanked their helmet straps against their jaws. Christiansen cut in with the Browning when the Kamanishi seemed to fill the sky. He went to his knees, firing with the muzzle of the gun swung into the perpendicular, the hot empties rattling on the deck and tumbling beneath his knees. He swept the aircraft from end to end with six hundred bullets before she was off target. She teetered away clumsily, and she was badly hurt.

But her second bomb had come aboard Exhibitor. It penetrated Number Six hatch, smashed through the hatch boards into the tea chests, kept on until it entered the lower 'tween-deck area and exploded. That blew a three-foot hole in the starboard side of the ship about four feet above the water line. Steel deck plates bulged and were torn by shrapnel; the big cargo booms were twisted askew, and two men of the Armed Guard crew, stationed in the port after gun tub, were flung down on deck.

The gunners were burned, dazed, and shocked. Still, they got back into the gun tub and cleared the piece for action. Down in Number Six, the bomb had started a roaring fire among the shattered tea chests. Mr. Christiansen came aft, his knees lacerated and bloody from the cuts he had suffered while he knelt and served the Browning. He now directed the water from four hoses into the hold, and the fire belched black smoke and steam and began to lessen.

The Kamanishi was back, swinging low over the river for a machine-gun strafe. The men who held the hoses stared up, transfixed, perfect targets on the exposed main deck. Then the portside gunners, the men who had been flung out of their tub by the bomb explosion, opened fire. The Kamanishi swerved, swerved more, and then was gone out of range and sight to the East.

Mr. Christiansen continued with his fire-control work. The blaze was out fifteen minutes later. Captain Wilson ordered the ship anchored so that an inspection could be made, and the radio operator was busy on the key, reporting to Calcutta what had happened.

A British fighter plane sent out from Calcutta intercepted 0-52, sluggish in the air and wobbly. The RAF pilot gave it a short burst and knocked it into the sea. It was towed to Chittagong and examined. Eight Japanese were in the crew, and all of them were dead. Some, from the condition of their wounds, had already been dead when the aircraft gave up the attack on *Exhibitor*.

Captain Wilson gave the order to Mr. Christiansen to repair the damage done by the bomb. It was not serious and was located above the water line. The chief officer and the deck gang built a large box of heavy planks, lined it with burlap and then secured it over the hole torn in the side of the ship. Cement was poured into the box and hardened, forming a seal. Mr. Christiansen was very pleased, and called each member of the deck gang into his room for a celebration drink of Scotch whisky.

Exhibitor remained at anchor during the afternoon while the chief engineer and his assistants checked the machinery. No major damage had been done to it, and Captain Wilson asked permission by radio to return to Calcutta for repairs. While he waited for Royal Navy clearance he made up the logbook for the day. He wrote:

"April 3. 11:16 A.M., anchor aweigh, proceeded. 12:20 P.M., attacked by plane. One bomb dropped, landing 20 yards off port quarter. 12:20 P.M., all AA guns opened fire. 12:26 P.M., one bomb was dropped into No. 6 hatch. Fire started. Plane driven off. 12:40 P.M., fire out.

"Day ends partly cloudy."

Captain Wilson was given clearance and took the ship back to Calcutta for repairs. Then he went down river again and made the run for Bombay. It was now clearly known that Japanese fleet units were in the Indian Ocean, and Captain Wilson asked maximum engine performance. He received it. *Exhibitor* held an average 17.5 knot speed steadily for 130 hours, came into Bombay, 2,300 miles from the mouth of the Hooghly, on April 18 without being

ANZIO. A slack moment off the Italian beachhead as the Liberty ship in the background discharges cargo into a shorebound barge and the *Luftwaffe* planes are busy somewhere else. The ship is the *Patrick Henry*, the first Liberty built. The guns in the foreground are Oerlikon twenty millimeters, famous antiaircraft weapons served by the United States Navy Armed Guard detachments aboard the merchant ships.

pursued or even sighted. *Exhibitor* was back Stateside with her precious chrome cargo in June, discharged it, and loaded once more for overseas.

But *Exmoor*, which had lain alongside her in Calcutta, was not as lucky. *Exmoor* had sailed with six other vessels in a slow convoy a few hours before *Exhibitor* headed for sea. The convoy held course southwest, toward Madras and Ceylon. It would take the ships at least a week's steaming time to make good the thousand sea miles to Ceylon, and the crews, without radio information about the enemy's activities, began to count each hour.

A Japanese fleet was already in the Bay of Bengal, bound for Ceylon and the capital city of Colombo. It was a powerful force that included three battleships, five aircraft carriers and several squadrons of cruisers and destroyers. They swung around Ceylon from the south and fanned out while the carrier-based planes took to the air. When the planes had finished their bombing runs on Colombo, the fleet closed with the shore and shelled the defenseless city.

A new course was set, northeast, after Colombo was left smashed and aflame. The destroyer screen cleared northernmost Ceylon by dawn, and early in the morning of April 6 the Japanese lookouts reported ships on the horizon. It was the Calcutta convoy.

There was nothing the convoy commander could do, or the shipmasters who sailed with him. They were trapped. The entire southern horizon was rimmed by the enemy fleet. Cruisers were being pulled out of the Japanese squadron columns. Flag hoists were shown; there was the greenish flicker of blinker messages. Three cruisers advanced, their range finders slowly revolving, the long, gray barrels of the guns coming around with them onto target.

The men of the convoy stood clammy-handed on deck. Here was death. The best that might be done was to keep from screaming when hit.

Captain Ragnar Frederick Eklund of the *Exmoor* waited in the bridge wing of his ship and watched the Japanese maneuver. He had already given his orders, warned the men. The muzzle flame was scarlet flicked with yellow, and the boom of the salvos almost as fast over the calm sea as the shell screech.

The first shell struck beneath the bridge, and took it from under Captain Eklund's feet. He was a portly man; he fell hard to the deck eight feet below. While he pulled himself upright, bloody, bruised, the next shells were entering the sides of the ship. The Japanese gunners were right on target. *Exmoor* was already low in the water, and very soon she would sink.

Captain Eklund hauled himself aft through the wreckage of the main house. He called out to his officers and all of them answered him, reported that as yet no man had been killed or seriously injured. The captain went back to what remained of the bridge. He stayed there while he gave the order to launch the lifeboats and abandon ship.

The Japanese shellfire continued. Captain Eklund could see other ships of the convoy as they sank; many men aboard them had been killed. Corpses floated around the suction slicks where the ships had gone, and wounded cried out about sharks. *Exmoor* was still a target. She sank fast. Captain Eklund got out of her when the main deck was awash.

He was pulled aboard a lifeboat and took his place on the stern sheets. Then he looked around at the Japanese cruisers. They were rejoining the fleet. The admiral in command did not want to spend any more ammunition.

"Row," Captain Eklund told the men in the boat. "There's land." He pointed toward Ceylon. "We can reach it. The land is not far."

Captain Eklund and the crew of *Exmoor* came back to the States and learned in New York what had happened right after their convoy was sunk. Another convoy of eight slow vessels had left the Hooghly two days later. It had no knowledge of the presence of the Japanese fleet and sailed

GET IT OUT AND ROLL IT. The *John S. Pillsbury*, with another sea-weary Liberty ship astern of her, discharges directly into Army trucks. This is in a Mediterranean port that has been badly hurt by enemy bombing. The Army trucks are backed up onto floating piers. When the Army Port Battalion men have finished loading, the trucks leave at once for the advanced areas.

NOT SO LUCKY. A German dive bomber has scored a direct hit on an American freighter. Fire spreading from the bomb blast amidships has ignited the explosive cargo, spraying the Sicilian sky with gaudy patterns. The photograph was taken from a Coast Guard manned combat transport. The photographer was in a very exposed position and must have handled his camera fast.

within easy range. All eight ships were sunk. Now, in April, 1942, the Japanese held a grip on the Indian Ocean that threatened passage across it to the Red Sea and the Suez Canal.

Japanese sea, land, and air forces, had swept within three months to the Indian frontier in Burma, and along the coast of New Guinea to Port Moresby, very close to the northern part of Australia. There was little left to stop new offensives. During the Battle of the Java Sea, fought in February, a large Dutch, American, and British force made up of cruisers and destroyers had been nearly wiped out by the Japanese, and only four American destroyers escaped it.

The American merchant marine was no longer able to sail the long traverses of the western Pacific without either great loss or strong escort. All available ships were also needed on the other side of the world. Doenitz conducted his U-boat campaign in the Caribbean and the Gulf of Mexico with frightful intensity. He kept many of his other craft in a gantlet around the British Isles, and off Iceland, and past the North Cape on the course to northern Russia. The Battle of the Atlantic would still decide the war and was of the utmost importance to the Allies.

chapter
4

NOW it was the Caribbean that was struck the hardest, as Doenitz sent his U-boats southward. The losses suffered there during May, June, July, and August of 1942 were greater than the terrible Atlantic toll. During two days alone, May 18 to May 20, eleven Allied ships were sunk. And in Washington it was calculated that 55 per cent of the shipping losses in the Caribbean were tanker vessels.

Doenitz had been ordered to stop the delivery of oil before it reached the American coastal ports and Great Britain and North Africa. Without high-octane gasoline and bunker fuel, the Allies could not last long. Aircraft carriers like those used by the United States Navy in the Coral Sea battle would be useless; the Royal Air Force planes attacking occupied Europe by the hundreds each night would stay on the ground; Montgomery's Eighth Army tanks and armored vehicles would rest motionless, ready targets for Rommel.

It was almost ridiculously simple for the U-boat commanders to carry out their orders. Most of the Allied oil came from the huge Lake Maracaibo field in Venezuela. Shallow-draft shuttle tankers carried the crude product to refineries on the offshore Dutch islands of Aruba and Curaçao. Then the various forms of refined oil were loaded into the big seagoing tankers for delivery at the ports of call.

The U-boat commanders were completely familiar with the tanker routes. Their sources of information regarding the Caribbean were flawless. Since the rise of Hitler to power, devoted Nazis had infiltrated the region and worked with deliberate care to create a spy network that reported to a special bureau in Berlin. Handsome young German businessmen arrived in Cuba, in Haiti, in the Dominican Republic, and throughout Central America. The firms they represented gave them large drawing accounts; they were very popular at the local swimming and tennis clubs. Many of them married into long-established Creole families and interested themselves in map making, photography, and short-wave radio.

U-boats took station off the seaward bar at Lake Maracaibo. They sank without interruption twelve shuttle tankers carrying crude-oil cargoes. But before that, as a flourish to open the campaign, a U-boat had surfaced close to the beach at Aruba. Her deck-gun crew thoroughly shelled the

Lago refinery and set the big complex afire. Another U-boat entered boldly into the inner harbor of Port of Spain, Trinidad, through the narrow passage known as the Dragons' Mouths. When she left, a loaded tanker was burning and a freighter had been sunk.

Enemy craft cruised the Caribbean at will. They came to the surface often during the daylight hours so that the crews could sunbathe and take calisthenics. Their attacks were usually made at night, as had been their practice in Atlantic waters. But here a ship's phosphorescent bow wash and wake radiantly marked her, starlight set her in silhouette, moonlight showed her in all her length.

U-boats waited off Trinidad, off Jamaica, and in the Windward Passage between Hispaniola and Cuba. This passage, taken by nearly all northbound tankers because it shortened steaming time, became a favorite zone of operation for the Nazis. Between the dark-green outthrust of Cape Dame Marie at the southerly end of the passage and Cape St. Nicholas at the northern end, ships were sunk with frightful regularity.

Haitian fishermen, venturing into the passage in their shabby little hardwood schooners, found at dawn a litter of bloodstained life jackets, a couple of gratings, an upturned boat, some candy bars. The rest, the sea and the sharks had taken. Reports were made faithfully when the fishermen returned to port. But there was little that the United States Navy could do.

Washington had announced in May that forty-three Liberty ships were finished and ready for operation. There had been, though, forty-four vessels sunk by U-boat action during the same month. The Caribbean Gulf Sea Frontier mustered a conglomerate force that included two destroyers and two patrol boats built for World War I duty, three submarines of the nearly obsolete S class, some really obsolete aircraft, and a number of yachts, tugs, and tenders all too slow to carry depth charges.

The American ship *San Pablo* had been loading bananas at night under the arc lights at Puerto Limon, Costa Rica, when she was torpedoed without warning or power to retaliate. Another American freighter, *Virginia*, was caught by a bracket of two torpedoes a mile from the whistle buoy at the entrance to Southwest Pass and the Mississippi River. She was outward-bound with a big deck load that contained aircraft, tanks, jeeps, and drums of high-octane gasoline. Her cargo weight and the current took her down fast; twenty-seven of her crew drowned, and only fourteen survived. The tanker *Benjamin Brewster* while at anchor at night off Galveston, Texas, was struck and sunk. Twenty-seven of her crew died—incinerated, blown apart, or drowned. This was in July, and the Nazi attack was to get worse.

Still, the Navy could not offer any further protection. Armed vessels that might have served as escort for Caribbean or Gulf convoys were needed in the Solomon Islands, around Iceland and Great Britain, and on the North Cape route to the northern Russian ports. The survivors from sunken ships accepted the fact and kept on going to sea. They closed their minds to the future and lived hour by hour, watch by watch, until they were back in port or death came for them.

The chaos of those spring and summer months of 1942 was so vast that there was never any accurate count made of the men and ships lost in action. Patrol craft tried to keep track, but the Caribbean region was much too large for accurate reconnaissance. Survivors drifted sometimes for weeks on life rafts or in boats without being sighted. Ship losses remained mysteries; no SOS messages were received from many, and no record of their destruction was found in captured German logbooks.

But during the latter part of June the Navy compiled and released a set of figures. There had been lost since Pearl Harbor a total of 350 ships. This was a frightening estimate. It meant that the United States and Great Britain must start at once on a greatly intensified shipbuilding program. Men were needed just as much as ships; that was granted too. The survivors coming into mainland ports were fewer by a hundred or so each month.

The government took public notice of the merchant seamen in an effort to help recruitment and to lift the morale of survivors. For the first time in the history of the country, awards were given to members of the oldest service for heroism in the face of the enemy. The Merchant Marine Distinguished Service Medal was designed in the form of the sixteen points of the compass, with a red, white, and blue ribbon. It was often recommended by shipmates, by the crews of other vessels who had witnessed a man's heroism, or by a Navy or Coast Guard or consular officer anywhere in the world.

The chairman of the Merchant Marine Awards Committee was Vice Admiral Arthur P. Fairfield, USN, Ret., and the executive secretary Captain Frank Rusk of the Maritime Commission and the War Shipping Administration. The committee also designed and awarded the Mariners Medal, given to men wounded in action, and later in the war, created the Meritorious Service Medal and the Gallant Ship award for vessels and their crews which had exceptionally distinguished themselves against the enemy.

Another award which was similar to that worn by men in the armed forces was known as the Merchant Marine Combat Bar. The symbolism used in its conception was simple. The horizontal stripe at the bottom was deep blue, signifying the sea; the narrow stripe at the center was red, for valor; and the uppermost stripe was light blue, for the sky.

The Combat Bar was awarded by the committee to a seaman whose vessel had been in direct enemy action. For every ship that the wearer had lost through enemy action, a silver star was bestowed and attached to the ribbon. Some men, before the war was over, wore three and four stars upon their ribbons.

Men were encouraged by the government and by their unions to wear these awards while ashore. Wearing them eliminated an enormous amount of friction and halted countless shoreside fights when the customary question was asked, "Why aren't you in uniform?" Fights still went on, but they would have occurred anyhow, and their origins will be explained in another part of this book.

The first man to receive the Merchant Marine Distinguished Service Medal was Edward F. Cheney, Jr. It was bestowed by President Roosevelt on October 8, 1942, at the White House. The award was prominently mentioned by the press, but was soon forgotten. There were too many great events of vital importance that held the public mind. Cheney's story, though, and the stories of some of the other

THEY WENT THAT WAY. The men, the guns, the ammunition begin to move away from this beachhead in southern France in 1944. The fighting has gone inland, northward. American Merchant Marine cargo ships and Coast Guard transports lie offshore. There are French troops among the United States Army units in the foreground.

men who were given the same medal, tell in microcosm what happened to so many during the early months of the war.

Cheney was a lanky, twenty-five-year-old sailor who came from Yeadon, Pennsylvania. He was serving as a quartermaster aboard the Atlantic Refining Company tanker *John D. Gill* and was at the wheel when she was struck by a U-boat torpedo on the night of March 12, off the Atlantic coast. The ship, loaded with bunker fuel, listed far over with the concussion.

Cheney was knocked from the wheel to the deck and stunned. When he got back to his feet, he knew that the ship was mortally hurt. She had been running entirely blacked out except for the narrow triangle of illuminated compass by which he steered. But now that was extinguished. All power was gone from the ship. Captain Allan B. Tucker could not ring the general-alarm bell or give the whistle-blast signal to abandon.

Oil from the smashed tanks lifted high in a gaseous fountain, then fell and filled the lifeboats that remained on the side where the torpedo had hit. Aft, along the main deck, there were quick little ripples of orange-yellow flame where gas and oil ignited. Captain Tucker told the men in the wheelhouse with him to abandon ship and to pass the word aft. But the men in the after part of the ship could not reach their boat stations; flame erupted from the main deck and soared ruddy over the mainmast.

Cheney left the wheelhouse and went to the port life raft, still secure in its steel frame. His boat station was aft, but the flame blocked him. Escape could only be made by swimming, or aboard the raft. He knocked up the pelican-hook ring that secured the raft; it slid into the water and kept on moving for about two hundred feet. Flame spread from the ship and out around the raft. A man who swam to it would very likely be burned to death.

Still, Cheney decided to make the attempt. It was the only way to stay alive, he said to the men who had gathered beside him at the life-raft frame. They shook their heads and pointed to the blazing oil. He took a long breath and dived into the sea.

He kept under the water as long as he could, swimming blindly toward the raft. When he was forced to the surface by his need for air, he was badly burned. Flames caught his hair, face, throat, arms, and hands. He dived and swam again until he reached the raft.

The wooden deck planks were aflame. But he crawled up on it. He splashed up water that put out the flame. His hands hurt him a great deal, and it was hard for him to hold them cupped around his mouth as he shouted to his shipmates who had dived after him.

A messboy named Perona was about to die. He was severely burned and could no longer swim or dive, Cheney saw. Cheney went back to him through the oil. When he had hauled Perona onto the raft, he returned for another man. His name was William Pryal, and Cheney called out to him to give him hope.

Cheney saved Pryal. He brought him to the raft and shoved him aboard it. Then he clambered on again himself. Pain dazed him, and yet, out in the oil, he saw six of his shipmates. Blinded by the heat, the flame, they could not find the raft.

Cheney gave them directions and they got aboard. Then

the raft started to drift back into the center of the blazing oil, drawn by the suction of the ship as she sank. That would be fatal, Cheney knew, but the rowlocks had been knocked off the raft. He showed the men how to make rowlocks with their hands. Some of them put their raw, blistered hands around the oar hafts, held the oars in place while others rowed. They pulled the raft clear while the ship sank, and until they were beyond the oil.

Rescue came for them ten hours later. Cheney talked to them during that time. He promised them that if they stayed calm they would be all right. None of them, despite their awful pain and thirst, tried to move or disturbed the equilibrium of the raft. They waited quietly, as Cheney had asked.

He spent three weeks in the hospital while on shore. He spent a month in convalescence after that with his wife and child. The doctors said he was fit then, and he returned to sea.

He joined another tanker, and she was torpedoed, too, off the Atlantic coast. Cheney suffered a broken rib and was not ashore as long. He was on his way to a new ship when President Roosevelt sent for him to come to Washington for his medal.

The next man to receive the decoration was Frank A. Santina. He was second officer aboard a freighter attacked in the Gulf of Mexico by a U-boat in broad daylight. The German craft came to the surface during the morning of May 26, 1942, and opened deck-gun fire, and the ship turned away at once at flank speed in an attempt to escape.

The ship was shelled for half an hour and then the U-boat released a torpedo that smashed a great, gaping hole

in the freighter's hull and tore the bridge apart. The order
was given to abandon ship. A boat carrying fifteen men got
clear. Santina was in the bow of a second boat which
held twenty men. He and the others were lowering themselves to the water when another torpedo hit. The explosion
was directly beneath their lifeboat.

The men were flung up and out from it into the sea. All
of them except Santina and a water tender named Kurt
Gonska were killed. Santina was severely wounded and
just about able to take care of himself and slowly swim.
But he saw that Gonska was so hurt that without help he
would drown.

Santina swam over to his shipmate. He towed him to
some wreckage that had been blasted from the ship. But
Santina realized they could not stay there long. Sharks
would get them, or Gonska would slip away and drown.
There were life rafts aboard the ship, and she might float
for a few minutes more.

Santina went to the ship, while the U-boat held fire and
men on her deck and in her conning tower watched him.
His slow, painful strokes took him into the thick spread of
bunker oil, through the wreckage, and past the bodies of his
shipmates. Then he hunkered up the steeply slanted side
plates of the freighter and got aboard. The first life raft he
reached had been jammed in the frame by explosion. The
other was the full length of the ship from where he
crouched.

He moved along the main-deck coamings, while beneath
him in the ship steam hissed and rumbled and steel
buckled. The ship was nearly finished. But he could not
hurry. He was very weak, and bunker oil was in his eyes,

made his hands and feet slippery. When he got to the raft he was spent and forced to rest before he groped for the pelican hook. The raft went smoothly and swiftly into the water, and he jumped after it, hands up over his eyes against the fuel oil.

He found the raft and boarded, then looked around as the ship reared and took her final plunge. Santina rowed with desperate strength out from the suction pull. He came alongside Gonska, almost comatose and too weak to give any help. Santina tugged at him and at last brought him onto the raft. He looked up then, over Gonska's sprawled body, and saw that the U-boat was gone.

He and Gonska lay on the raft in the blazing Gulf sunlight through the rest of the day and into the night. That night a ship found them and the other survivors and took them to port. Santina, when he had recovered from his wounds, went back to sea, but left his medal ashore.

There were, after Cheney and Santina, only a few other men to be so decorated for heroism during the ordeal of those first months of the war. The awards committee was very careful in its selections. But each of the stories cannot be told in detail. One must be mentioned because of the exceptional circumstance in which four men aboard the same ship were all decorated for gallantry.

The Distinguished Service Medal given to Hawkins Fudske was bestowed posthumously, and received by his wife, Mrs. Dagny Fudske, of Brooklyn, New York. The reason should be plain: Mr. Fudske, chief officer aboard a tanker sunk off the Atlantic coast, gave his life to save his shipmates. The vessel was attacked by a U-boat while in

LONELY LOOKOUT. Two Armed Guard gunners stand watch beside their weapons in the after gun tub of a Liberty ship during a North Atlantic storm. The force of the wind can be told by the spindrift torn from the wave crests.

ballast and bound south to take cargo.

The trio who survived to be decorated were the chief engineer, Thomas J. McTaggert, Fireman Arthur Lauman, and Able Seaman Charles D. Richardson. They returned to sea when the ship in which they had served with Mr. Fudske was saved and brought into port for repairs.

The U-boat attacked at night. No warning was given. There was only the bright crease of muzzle flame. Then shells came whining aboard the tanker, crashed into her hull and deckhouses and bridge. Mr. McTaggert got an order from the bridge for all possible speed. Maybe, in the darkness, the ship might evade the U-boat.

Pursuit lasted for more than two hours. The German craft closed steadily, running on the surface and using her deck gun and then her Maxim machine guns. The captain was killed in the riddled wheelhouse, along with several other men. Mr. Fudske took over as acting captain. But the ship was being given terrible punishment, and she could not keep her course much longer.

The Nazi bombardment had started fires on deck, among the deck cargo, in the crew's quarters, and below. When a shell smashed the steering engine and the ship yawed wildly without any control from her helm, it was time to abandon. Mr. Fudske gave the order from the bridge.

It was passed by speaking tube to the engine room. McTaggert was there with his second assistant engineer, the oiler, and the wiper on watch. He kept the second assistant with him and sent the other two men topside to their boat stations. Then he went into the fireroom to talk with the fireman.

Arthur Lauman was sixty years old and had spent most

of his life at sea. He was quietly tending his fires when Mc-Taggert told him to knock off; the ship was being abandoned. Lauman said, "All right, sir." He had been alone here since the first Nazi shell came aboard, and now the fireroom floor was littered with debris. There was a ten-foot-long piece of six-inch pipe torn from aloft out of the smokestack casing, and a considerable amount of twisted, explosive-ripped metal had come down with it. Steam from punctured pipes stung at Lauman when he bent down to regulate the furnace burners, and before he was ready to leave, another shell hit the stack uptake, and bunker fuel was ignited. Lauman could not get out of the fireroom into the engine room.

He climbed up the side plates of the engine-room skylights to deck. Below him, burning bunker fuel was spilling across the fireroom floor. Shell fragments, machine-gun bursts, and clouds of steam made the skylights very uncomfortable. Lauman wiggled up, out, onto deck, and went to his boat station.

McTaggert and the second assistant engineer were still in the engine room. They took the main engine out of gear, so that if any man were swept astern of the ship, he would not be macerated by the propeller blades. They closed down all pump and fuel valves, and the generator, and the condenser. It was their intention to come back here later if the ship could be saved. When the work was done, they lunged into the fireroom, leaped above the flame, and scrambled on deck in the way taken by Lauman.

But there was only one lifeboat left intact. That was midships, and the survivors gathered around her under the command of Mr. Fudske. She was swung overside already, and now men began to lower away on the falls.

The U-boat had come very close. Shells were sent methodically into the ship with rapid salvos. Mr. Fudske was wounded; a shell fragment nearly severed an arm. He kept on working, hauling at fall rope. The boat took the water. Men boarded her as Mr. Fudske gave the order. Another shell hit, and he was mortally wounded.

He crouched almost prone and shook his head when men tried to help him. Those who heard what he said remembered the words. He told them, "Never mind me, fellows. Get the boat away." Before they were all in the boat, he was dead.

Mr. McTaggert took command of the boat and she was rowed away from the ship. The Nazi machine gunners chopped at her with hundreds of rounds. Men lay down on the floor boards at McTaggert's order, but the gunners kept the boat as target. The boat hull was a poor shield; it was repeatedly punctured.

McTaggert told the men to leave the boat and submerge in the water, the boat between them and the Nazis. He went first and exposed himself to Nazi fire so that the others would fully understand what they must do. They followed him, and together they pulled the boat around and submerged neck-deep.

Then the U-boat commander put a torpedo into the ship. That exploded against the side of the ship right behind McTaggert's group. Men were flung sprawling upward out of the sea by the concussion. They flopped back weak and stunned, most of them unable to take care of themselves. But the lifeboat still floated. The U-boat commander, satisfied with his work, had taken off, the wake dim on the night sea.

For a while, until the men had regained their strength, Mr. McTaggert waited. He went aboard the lifeboat and gave a hand to the weak. All of the group were brought into the boat, and McTaggert cheered them by pointing out that the ship had not yet sunk. He kept the boat close to the ship during the night, and with dawn he sighted a number of other survivors from the crew. They floated around the ship in life jackets or hung onto planks from the deck-cargo dunnage. He went to them in the boat and saved them.

Among the men he took aboard the lifeboat was an able-bodied sailor named Charles D. Richardson. While the ship had been under attack, Richardson had served with the Navy gun crew. He was wounded by a shell fragment in the back, but two of the Navy gunners were much more severely hurt. Richardson tended to the pair when the order came to abandon ship.

Richardson carried one and then the other to the side rail of the ship. The best he could do for them was to pitch them over it into the sea. But he joined them there. Both were too badly wounded to swim or keep themselves afloat.

Richardson, despite his own wound, took one upon his back and told the other man to clasp him by the neck. So burdened, he began to swim toward the lifeboat. The Nazi shellfire was intense, and ricochet fragments lashed whining around them, kicking up gouts of spray into Richardson's face. His progress was very slow, and in the light of the fires on deck, before he heard the man on his back scream, he saw sharks.

There were several, drawn by the scent of blood and fast to strike. Richardson wore his sailor's knife in a scabbard at his right hip. He reached around and cleared it and

DOUBLE LASHING. The bosun and deck gang of a Liberty ship secure a lifeboat while the sea roils white over the side. The boats are carried swung outboard for imme-

diate lowering in case of emergency, and a single wave
could snatch them from the davits.

fought the sharks while the sea in which he swam pulsated terribly with the shock of shellfire and then the torpedo. And all the while the two men hung upon him.

The knife was sharp. It had a broad, heavy blade. Richardson struck with it, and struck with it. But the man on his back was pulled away and taken by the sharks. When they were done, they returned for him and the other man. Richardson fought them in the embrace of the wounded gunner who still held to his neck. He won. The shark left them. At dawn they were hauled into the lifeboat by Mr. McTaggert and were given great care. They knew they would live.

The ship was sighted after dawn; her greasy columns of smoke lifted high above the horizon. A rescue vessel picked up the occupants of McTaggert's lifeboat and they were put ashore. Mr. McTaggert, though, was unhappy over the abandonment of the ship. He talked with the Navy about her, and it was agreed that a salvage attempt would be made.

A Navy salvage crew went out with McTaggert to the last known position of the ship. She was still afloat and still aflame and carried a very bad list. They boarded her, rigged hoses and used other fire-fighting equipment. When the fires were extinguished, McTaggert entered the engine room. He checked the engines and reported to the Navy officer in command that the ship could be sailed under her own power.

Manned by Navy personnel, but with McTaggert at the throttle, the tanker steamed into port. Temporary repairs were made there under McTaggert's supervision. Then she sailed for her home port, a thorough overhaul, and further service.

It was claimed without dispute in a number of dockside saloons that men like McTaggert gave Scotch engineers a good name.

THE FIRST. It took 244 days to build *Patrick Henry*. But construction time for the Liberty ships was later reduced to seventeen days from keel laying until launching. The total number built was 2,710.

chapter
5

THE decisive months of the war were those of the spring and summer of 1942, when American merchant seamen were asked to take such terrible risks at sea, and the ship-loss rate remained at an average of 20,-000 tons a day. The government had already begun building a tremendous fleet of new ships and was to spend on them three billion dollars. But all of the heroism, endurance, and skill of men like McTaggert could not keep the ships in operation. Over 200,000 men had to be recruited for crews, or the war effort would collapse.

President Roosevelt had created in February the War Shipping Administration, which took over the functions of the Maritime Commission and also the control of mer-

HOW IT WAS DONE. Prefabrication in a Liberty shipyard. Winches are in the foreground, ventilator hoods past

them, and behind them the ships with deckhouses already installed.

chant marine operations of every sort. An important part of the vast new administrative structure was the Recruitment and Manning Organization, under the direction of Marshall E. Dimock. His major concern was to go out and get men for the ships, then establish training centers.

A wide-flung publicity campaign was started to induce old-timers to return to sea. Rear Admiral Emory S. Land, USN, Ret., had been appointed head of the War Shipping Administration, and he was unremitting in his personal appeals to former seamen in speeches and over the radio. Captain Edward Macauley, Deputy Administrator and another retired Navy officer with a distinguished record, concentrated upon the training problems and relations with the various maritime unions.

The War Shipping Administration had absorbed the 131 operators of ships which sailed under the American flag. They were now "general agents" for the government, and the entire fleet of merchant ships, those in commission as well as those being built, were allocated among them. There had been at first some reluctance expressed by shipping officials who were afraid of government interference in operation of their vessels. But the terms granted them for ship handling were generous; they were paid by the government for each operational phase—maintenance, loading, discharge, fueling and victualing, repairs, and manning.

The shipping companies held in their files the names of thousands of men who had worked for them in years past. They sent out appeals to the former seamen or turned the lists over to the WSA. For a time, in the glow of high-pressure publicity, merchant seamen were made out to be romantic figures. Men were startled, if not amused, and so were their wives, friends, and employers.

But most of them went back to sea. They gave up jobs in shipyards and steel mills where they were untouched by the Selective Service Act. Some few of them were released by the Army for sea duty, and others had been away from the ships so long they had forgotten a great deal about work aboard. But masters, mates, and engineers were patient with them, and out to sea they learned to steer again, and to clean burners and open and shut the right valves.

They became very seagoing, renewed their tattoos when ashore, and sported white cotton caps cocked at an angle, tight-fitting dungarees, and blue flannel shirts, with their union emblems on the shirt pockets or caps, sometimes both. A number of their wives had cut out and sent on to them an editorial printed in *The New York Times*, and this they read to bartenders, to shipmates, to anybody who would listen. It was really belated recognition on the part of the public for what still continued at sea:

"Tankermen and other men of the American merchant marine literally go through fire to carry supplies to our armed forces in remote lands. Each week they are pulled or washed up out of the sea, after incredible hardships, or after death amid vast stretches of flaming oil. Quietly, when their burns are healed, their long thirst or hunger satisfied, the survivors slip out of port again with more supplies, with more oil and gasoline for our fighting planes and tanks. Many come through three or four sinkings, yet do not hesitate when new ships are ready. No one turns in the street to admire their uniforms. They wear no uniform. No one steps up to the bar to buy them drinks. No moist-eyed old ladies turn to them in the subway to murmur "God bless you." The cop on the beat, gentle with the tipsy soldier or the unsteady gob, is apt to put his nightstick to the britches of a merchant sailor who has tippled heavily in the town's bars to celebrate his rescue from the sea."

All of the maritime unions had come strongly to the defense of their members in any case where there were allegations of Navy discrimination or unfair treatment of survivors when men were brought into a port overseas by a rescue vessel. There was actually no difference in survivor treatment during the first months of the war. Both merchant seamen and their Navy shipmates of the Armed Guard were shown equal lack of care, particularly in the Caribbean.

Trinidad had come to be known as "Torpedo Junction," and the survivors from sunken ships arrived daily in Port of Spain. They were allowed to go barefoot and half-naked. There was nothing like adequate medical care. Wounds and burns festered. One man, who for six nights in a row, exactly at midnight, had seen ships of a convoy sunk, the last his own, was finally offered a pair of woolen golf socks by a well-intentioned local citizen.

When conditions were corrected in Port of Spain and other Caribbean and Gulf rescue ports, it was mainly owing to the action taken by the seamen's unions. The biggest and most alert and effective of them was the National Maritime Union. It was run by Joe Curran, a large and rough-voiced man who looked with critical regard at the new regulations being established by the Navy and the Coast Guard, and who had small liking for shipowners because of his early years of union struggle.

The National Maritime Union had entered the war with a membership of about 75,000 men and women, the latter stewardesses and waitresses aboard passenger liners. The union greatly expanded during the war, and its vigorous weekly paper, *The Pilot*, carried at the top of the front page the slogan "We Keep 'Em Sailing." This was fact. The NMU, throughout the four years of the war, gained a fine record.

Members wore jauntily a big, gold-trimmed device which was known commonly as "the junior G-man badge," and torpedo-shaped pins were issued to each man who had lost a ship through enemy action. The union headquarters on Seventeenth Street between Eighth and Ninth Avenues in New York City was kept open day and night. Men congregated by the hundreds on the sidewalk outside it and in the main hiring hall.

The NMU was the only seagoing union to accept Negroes as members. Broad Jamaican accents could be heard as shipmate hailed shipmate, and in some groups made up of Puerto Ricans the language was rapid-fire Spanish. Moving in and out of the hall and from group to group, almost as though blind, were men with blank eyes and faces. whose hands twitched with uncontrollable tension. They were the recently torpedoed. Curran and other union officials often took them in charge, turned them over to a psychiatrist the union had hired.

Then there were the drunks, "the live ones," just in from a ship with a big pay-off and a larger thirst. There were a number of lean, hungry, and equally thirsty members ready to claim that they had once sailed with the new arrivals,

TWO CRANES AND A MIDSHIPS SECTION. A Liberty ship is about to receive a very important part of her superstructure.

and to conduct a tour of the Chelsea bars. The phrase for it was "to rig the towline," and the words had sharp meaning. Sometimes a thousand-dollar pay-off was spent in the space of a day and night.

But the majority of the men were quiet, almost remote from each other as they stood in the big hiring hall and listened to the dispatchers' voices over the microphone, studied the ships listed on a blackboard that covered an entire wall. Then, the decision made, they stepped forward to the dispatcher's window, their union books in their hands. This was a rotary hiring system, and the man who had been on the beach the longest was given the vessel of his choice.

With his book accepted and the assignment to the ship made, the man stepped aside and the line closed behind him. He nodded to a couple of former shipmates, wondering if he would meet them aboard the new vessel. Then his own concerns occupied him. He thought about his seabag and his suitcase, and about whether he would pass medical inspection despite injuries received in the last torpedoing, and about what would happen at sea during this voyage.

The same atmosphere of both noise and quiet concentration pervaded the hall of the Seamen's International Union in Brooklyn. This was a smaller organization, affiliated with the AFL instead of the CIO, but very active and with a growing membership. Nearly all of the men wore the cocky white cotton caps, and in their talk frequently mentioned West Coast ports. They were for the most part West Coast men, their union affiliated with the Sailors' Union of the Pacific. The head of their union was a stocky and wily man named Paul Hall, but a great deal of their respect went to Harry Lundeberg, who had organized the Sailors' Union and was famous on the West Coast for his militancy.

There were at the start of the war twenty-two maritime unions, some of them company dominated and not fully representative of the wishes of the rank and file. The three mentioned above remained the most powerful and gave great, constructive help to the manning of the ships. Wide divergencies of personal characteristics and political and economic beliefs existed among their leaders, though. They were only agreed upon one point; neither the Navy nor the government through the WSA was going to take over control of their membership. It was often said in various Washington offices during the first part of the war that the seamen's unions carried on a private war with the Navy.

This was true in part. It was also true, curiously and sadly enough, that to some extent the Navy allowed it to happen. History is cloudy as to just what brought the conflict about. There is no doubt that a whispering campaign was begun and spread to the newspapers and national magazines. It accused merchant seamen of being cowards, slackers, men interested in nothing but the size of their pay-offs.

When the effect of the campaign was found to be seriously hurting shipboard morale, Frank Knox, the Secretary of the Navy, and other high-ranking Navy officers attempted to stop it and at last succeeded. The charges about refusing to work cargo unless overtime was paid and unwillingness to man guns during enemy attack were emphatically denied. The fact was stressed that at all times while at sea, merchant marine personnel were under Navy orders; they could be called before courts-martial for disobedience and failure to perform crucial duty.

Wages were also cited and comparisons made between what was paid Navy ratings and merchant seamen performing similar duty. Here is a wage comparison:

"The Navy bluejacket's pay started at $50 per month; the merchant seaman's at $100 for a 44-hour week (85 cents for every hour after that), plus $100 war bonus in the Atlantic, plus various sums around $100 for each different combat area entered. On 15 Mar. 1943, this last bonus, greatly to the indignation of the National Maritime Union, was commuted to a flat rate of $125 per man for every air raid occurring when the ship was in port, whether or not the ship was hit. Although the merchant seaman was not paid when on the beach, continuous employment was guaranteed during the war. He did not, of course, receive the family allowances and retirement pay of the naval seaman. Some very erroneous figures of 'average wages' of merchant seamen, based apparently on their loafing half the year, were given out. The *Pilot* on 17 Sept. 1943, began agitating for a 40-hour week and overtime for all work on Saturdays, Sundays and holidays."

This was printed as a footnote on page 299 of *The Battle of the Atlantic*, by Rear Admiral Samuel Eliot Morison, USNR, Ret., who served throughout the war in the capacity of historian for the Navy. His comparison of wages and his conclusions drawn from it have been disputed and revised by several sources. The consensus at present is that the Navy bluejacket and the merchant seaman, one way or another, through immediately paid bonuses or pension rights received later, were given pretty much equal sums of money. The issue may seem almost laughable now, but back in the crucial months of 1942, it was very serious.

Merchant seamen found that they were no longer romantic figures, but were to be regarded as slackers, dollar-chasers, and Reds. These allegations, repeated almost endlessly, drove a large proportion of the merchant marine personnel to implacable dislike of the Navy. Thousands of men quit the ships in disgust that was mixed with dismay over the losses suffered at sea. (Joe Curran in the NMU *Pilot*, April 2, 1943, stated that 23,000 seamen were ashore in the Port of New York.) Those who stayed took as a ready target the members of the Navy Armed Guard with whom they were now forced to live aboard ship.

It was discovered that in each Armed Guard detachment a petty officer, a coxswain, or a bosun's mate was assigned to survey the unlicensed personnel of the merchant crew, create friendly relations, and learn all he could about those who might express "Communist leanings." Furthermore, the regular crew discovered that their ship had been extensively invaded—if not completely claimed—by the Armed Guard.

Quarters were already cramped as a result of safety and blackout regulations. Now the Armed Guard, young men, practically all of them in their teens, roamed the passageways, made the decks noisy, seemed to be always on the ladders, and in their messrooms created weird shambles with cereals, canned milk, catsup, and sugar. There were inevitable fights, and chasms of distrust were widened beyond repair by the Armed Guard commanders, ensigns and lieutenants junior grade, nearly all of whom were in their early twenties and making their first voyages to sea.

They had their own problems with the masters, the chief

TANKER: ATLANTIC COAST, 1942. A German U-boat has just put a torpedo into the vessel approximately amidships on the port side. Her tanks, filled with viscous fuel oil, are ruptured at the point of impact. Flame has begun to erupt, and oil spreads out across the sea. The ship's entire cargo may catch fire at any instant, make her an enormous torch, and incinerate her crew.

officers, and the radio operators. Safety regulations were part of their responsibility, and the encoding and decoding of all messages, the handling of visual signals. Some masters were unduly stubborn about handling the encoding and decoding themselves; others would not permit Armed Guard officers on the bridge or in the wheelhouse. Chief mates warned the Armed Guard away from deck gear and cargo spaces, denied them use of any ship's stores, saw that

Navy paint was used on the gun tubs, and even Navy-issued chipping hammers. Radio operators were a bit more unbending, but among their number were men who swore solemnly that the Navy operators assigned to work with them could not take or send a message in plain language.

Most of the bad feeling between the merchant marine crews and the Armed Guard detachments happened early in the war and was concentrated aboard the Liberty ships. The Liberties were the great cargo-haulers of the war and also served as troop transports and tankers. But they were never known by their crews to be comfortable or "a home away from home." Men were jammed into their living quarters in the same way cargo filled their holds and deck spaces.

The Liberty carried the formal identification of EC-2, which meant "emergency cargo vessel." Her design was an adaptation of a British freighter type called the Sunderland. She was, though, of welded construction instead of riveted plate. Her power plant was extremely simple, old style triple-expansion steam engines which gave only 2,500 horsepower and a loaded speed of eleven knots. But they could be handled by inexperienced engineers and repaired easily in British yards, where the type was well known. Her cargo gear—booms, winches, and capstans—was also simple and old-fashioned. Men returning to sea from years of shore life would recognize and readily use it.

Because of her slowness and clumsy, boxlike design, which meant that she could not run by herself and must move in convoy, acceptance of the Liberty shipbuilding program initiated for the British in 1940 was vigorously protested in Washington. It was only after months of insistence on the part of Admiral Land that the order was given for the type to be put in construction.

She was 441 feet 6 inches in over-all length. Her loaded water line length was 428 feet. Her extreme beam was 57 feet, and her loaded draft 27 feet 6 inches. Her tonnage was 7,176 gross, and 10,500 dead weight. (Pilots sometimes protested that Liberties were loaded so deeply they had to step down to board them from their cutters.)

The Liberty was built with two decks, three masts, five cargo holds, a single propeller, and small living quarters for her crew. Her normal crew complement was forty-four men, to which was added in the latter part of 1942 the Armed Guard detachment, which usually numbered from ten to twenty men. The armament was either one or two cannon, commonly of three-inch, fifty-caliber type, several twenty-millimeter Oerlikon antiaircraft guns, and lighter machine guns.

Men of the Armed Guard detachments lived in tightly packed living spaces in the main, midships house with the regular ship personnel, and aft, close to their cannon. This weapon was mounted on the poop; communications were maintained by telephone between the gunners stationed there and those midships and forward. It was one of the major complaints of the merchant seamen that the gunners talked continuously with each other over the telephone in unnecessarily loud voices, and that their conversations rarely made sense.

This, again, may seem laughable, but it was not to a man suffering from torpedo nerves. When off watch, he lay in a narrow steel bunk which was one of four in the cramped room. It contained four steel lockers, a wooden bench, a

A GOOD MAN. The ship's carpenter moves down onto the main deck with a foamite hose bucking in his hands. The ladder on which he stands is twisted by the torpedo,

wastebasket, and a single porthole which was sealed shut and painted gray in accordance with blackout regulations. The door out into the passageway bore a plywood panel in its lower half. This was stenciled with luminous paint, and the stencil read: EMERGENCY ESCAPE PANEL, and, below that, KICK OUT.

The man with torpedo nerves who tried to sleep found himself staring fascinated at the kickout panel. He knew—he had checked over and over again—just how many seconds it would take him to get from his bunk through that door, along the passageway, up the ladder, onto the boat

and the deck he sprays has bent under the intense heat. The carpenter won. He saved the ship.

deck and to his boat station in case of disaster. When the ship was in heavy weather and a wave struck its side, he started up, grasping his shoes and his life jacket, ready to go, and his watchmates did not laugh at him, pretended not to have seen and to be still asleep.

There was at least one man in every crew who could not sleep at all between sundown and dusk, the usual time of U-boat attack. He wandered around the passageways, wearing his life jacket, carrying an escape kit that contained his papers, his money, some cigarettes and candy bars. He jumped at the slightest sound, and quivered so when he sat in the messroom that he slopped coffee from the mug he gripped with both hands.

Loud sound of any sort was a cause of extreme agitation for these men. They could not forget the other sounds, the crashing and the rendering which were destruction and death, the end of the ship. Masters protested to Armed Guard officers, and gradually the young gunners learned the way of the sea in wartime and reduced their telephone conversations to what made strict shipboard sense.

Then there were two instances of very close cooperation between the merchant crew and the Armed Guard while in

THE SHIP HE SAVED. When the carpenter put out the fire, his shipmates brought the vessel into port.

action; word was carried ashore and did a great deal of good to make shipboard relations better. Those were never completely straightened out, and throughout the war friction existed. But, at least, men came to respect one another and in many cases were proud to use the term shipmate in its real sense.

The first instance of unqualified response to common danger occurred when the freighter *Columbian* was pursued by a U-boat on June 16, 1942, just at dusk. She was bound from New York to Basra with cargo for the Soviet Union, and was five days out of Trinidad and seven hundred miles off the Brazilian coast at the time the submarine was sighted. The U-boat lay on the surface ahead. Captain Edwin E. Johnson of *Columbian* immediately changed course and began evasive tactics.

But the U-boat stayed in pursuit although Captain Johnson changed course twice before darkness and twice afterward. The last course alteration was at midnight, and while it was being executed, the chief mate spotted the German craft almost under the stern of the ship. The chief mate stood on the wheelhouse topside, chosen as the best possible lookout station, and he called to Captain Johnson, below on the bridge, "Hard right! There she is!"

Captain Johnson instantly gave the order to the sailor at the wheel. The ship swung and barely missed striking the U-boat with her propeller and rudder. But Ensign Merrill R. Stone, Jr., in command of the Armed Guard, was able to bring the four-inch gun on the poop to bear at point-blank range. A shell from it hit the U-boat.

There was a sharp-flaring sheet of flame upward from the craft. The crew of the *Columbian* put another shell aboard her, and two of the Oerlikon gunners opened up their peices. No return fire came from the U-boat; her deck gun and machine guns were unmanned.

The U-boat escaped without further injury, though, and in his report the master of *Columbian* stated, "The last I could see of him, he was lying still at right angles to our course, and seemed to be getting low in the water."

It was the report made by Ensign Merrill that marked the significance of the encounter. He wrote: "Cooperation between officers and crew of the *Columbian* and the Armed Guard unit was the chief factor in the success of this engagement, because by the proper maneuvering of the ship, we were able to get a good range on the submarine."

The second instance of shipmates proving themselves to each other in action was wholly tragic, contained no element of possible victory. It is remembered because of the heroism displayed; the name of Edwin O'Hara is famous among the cadets of the United States Merchant Marine Academy at Kings Point, New York, where O'Hara was a cadet in his time, before he went to serve on *Stephen Hopkins*.

She was a Liberty ship under the command of Captain Paul Buck. Her course was shaped from Capetown across the South Atlantic to Paramaribo when on the morning of September 27, 1942, she met a pair of German surface raiders. These were motorships. One, known as raider *J*, was the ex-*Cairo* and of 5,000 tons. The other was the 7,800-ton *Tannenfels*, a blockade-runner.

The weather was hazy, but at noon the German ships closed quickly with *Stephen Hopkins*, and all three cleared for action. Captain Buck turned his vessel so that the four-inch cannon carried aft could be trained against *J*, the raider. This was the more powerfully armed German vessel, and the Armed Guard officer, Ensign Kenneth M. Willett, USNR, concentrated his fire upon her.

Mr. Willett took charge of the four-inch gun and served, at a range of a thousand yards or less, thirty-five shells. Most of these struck the raider along the water line and gave her great trouble. But Mr. Willett was severely injured, suffering shrapnel wounds of the stomach. Then a shell from the German raider penetrated the four-inch magazine and it exploded. Mr. Willett went down on deck and gave a hand to casting off the life rafts.

The combat had been uneven from the start, and the men who served the *Stephen Hopkins'* guns must have recognized right along how it would end. Raider *J* carried one three-inch and six 5.9-inch guns. These were mounted in turrets or behind shields and were handled by a central fire-control system. *Tannenfels* lacked heavy guns forward; she kept bow-on to the Liberty ship and raked her with intensive machine-gun fire.

This was hotly returned by the men who worked the lighter weapons aboard *Stephen Hopkins*. An Office of Naval Intelligence Survivors' Report states:

"The second mate, Joseph E. Lehman, who was in charge of the two 37-mm guns forward, put round after round into the larger raider, until his ammunition handlers were killed and the gun platform wrecked. The chief mate, Richard Macskowski, who was shot high in the chest and in the left forearm, continued to direct and rally his men and to advise the master to keep the ship turning with her stern bearing on the enemy, although he was losing considerable blood due to his great activity. He continued to rally his men from a reclining position on the deck and then got to his feet again with the aid of an ordinary seaman, so as to be better able to discharge his duties."

Edwin O'Hara, who was nineteen years old and an engine-room cadet, was below when the Germans opened fire. Two of the men who worked there were killed, and O'Hara went on deck to his battle station with the crew of the four-inch gun. He left the gun tub after the German shell exploded the magazine and accompanied Mr. Willett to the main deck.

One of the ship's boilers had been struck, and she could barely maintain headway. Her radio aerial was smashed. Incendiary shells set the main deckhouse afire. Then a shell destroyed the steering engine. The fight had been going on for almost three hours. Captain Buck passed the order to abandon.

Mr. Willett stood bloody while he helped lower away the mizzen life rafts. He waved to his men to get aboard them. There was a high wind blowing that roused heavy seas, and only one of the lifeboats was undamaged. But O'Hara went back to the four-inch gun.

He knew that five shells had escaped the explosion. They lay scattered on the gun-tub deck. He picked up the first fifty pounds' worth of death, slipped it in the breech, trained around on *Tannenfels*, checked his range and bearing, and fired.

The raider was burning fore and aft and about to sink. O'Hara did not bother with her. He kept on at *Tannenfels*. When he had fired the fifth shell and was stepping back from the recoil, he was caught by a direct hit.

The only surviving officer of *Stephen Hopkins* was the second engineer, George D. Cronk. He saw O'Hara die, and with the steward's help he took the lifeboat away as the ship bucked, rolled, dived into 2,200 fathoms. Then he gathered the survivors and began the voyage to Brazil.

They were not bothered. *Tannenfels* was busy taking off the raider crew. Still, there were no charts and no navigating instruments aboard the lifeboat. Mr. Cronk made the two-thousand-mile voyage by guesswork. The original count in the boat was nineteen men; nine of those died. Mr. Cronk brought the boat ashore just north of Rio de Janeiro on October 27, 1942, and made his report. *Stephen Hopkins* had lost, all told, forty-two men.

It was not until the final months of 1942 and the period in which *Stephen Hopkins* was destroyed that the number of new ships built exceeded the losses at sea. *Patrick Henry* was the first Liberty ship built. She was launched on September 27, 1941, at the Bethlehem Steel Corporation's Fairfield yard in Baltimore and delivered at the end of December. She had required 244 days of construction work, but this was reduced for later Liberty ships.

Shipyards were in production all over the country, and men like Henry J. Kaiser took a direct part in their operation. Mass methods were used, and women and high-school students became welders, electricians, pipe fitters. During 1942, American yards turned out 646 freighters, among which were 597 Liberty ships; the rest were tankers and other types. Tanker production, though, was still behind losses, and the War Shipping Administration acted to increase it.

By May, 1943, tanker deliveries reached as many as fourteen or fifteen vessels a month. Liberty-ship construction time was cut down until in 1944 the average was forty-two days for a fully commissioned ship. Production then remained steadily ahead of ship losses.

But the public was not aware until after the war of how very close the nation had been to defeat during the first months of the struggle. Memoranda which had been passed between General George C. Marshall, Chief of Staff of the United States Army, and Admiral Ernest J. King, Commander in Chief of the United States Fleet, were finally released. General Marshall wrote on June 19, 1942, to Admiral King:

"The losses by submarines off our Atlantic seaboard and in the Caribbean now threaten our entire war effort. The following statistics bearing on the subject have been brought to my attention.

"Of the 74 ships allocated to the Army for July by the War Shipping Administration, 17 have already been sunk. Twenty-two percent of the bauxite fleet has already been destroyed. Twenty percent of the Puerto Rican fleet has been lost. Tanker sinkings have been 3.5 percent per month of tonnage in use.

"We are all aware of the limited number of escort craft available, but has every conceivable improvised means been brought to bear on this situation? I am fearful that another month or two of this will so cripple our means of transport that we will be unable to bring sufficient men and planes to bear against the enemy in critical theaters to exercise a determining influence on the war."

Admiral King made his reply on June 21, and wrote:

"1. I have long been aware, of course, of the implications of the submarine situation as pointed out in your memorandum of 19 June. I have employed—and will continue to employ—not only regular forces but also such improvised means as give any promise of usefulness. However, it is obvious that the German effort is expanding more rapidly than our defense, and if we are to avoid disaster not only the Navy itself but also all other agencies concerned must continue to intensify the anti-submarine effort.

"2. As you are aware, we had very little in the way of anti-submarine forces in the Atlantic at the outbreak of the war except the fleet destroyers which were committed to troop escort duty and other services that made them unavailable for the protection of shipping in general. We had to improvise rapidly and on a large scale.

"We took over all pleasure craft that could be used and sent them out with makeshift armament and untrained crews. We employed for patrol purposes aircraft that could not carry bombs, and planes flown from school fields by student pilots. We armed our merchant ships as rapidly as possible. We employed fishing boats as volunteer lookouts. The Army helped in the campaign of extemporization by taking on the civil aviation patrol. These measures were worth something, but the heavy losses that occurred up to the middle of May on our east coast give abundant proof, if proof were needed, that they were not an answer to our problem."

Admiral King went on to describe in the memorandum the efforts being made to increase the production of submarine chasers. He mentioned the borrowing of escort ves-

sels from the British, and the establishment of the first convoy system from Key West northward along the Atlantic
coast. Then he stated:

> "Though we are still suffering heavy losses outside
> the east coast convoy zone the situation is not hope-
> less. We know that a reasonable degree of security can
> be obtained by suitable escort and air coverage. The sub-
> marines can be stopped only by wiping out the German
> building yards and bases—a matter which I have been
> pressing with the British, so far with only moderate
> success. But if all shipping can be brought under escort
> and air cover our losses will be reduced to an acceptable
> figure. I might say in this connection that escort is not
> just *one* way of handling the submarine menace; it is
> the *only* way that gives any promise of success."

Admiral King detailed next the various types of planes
and small local patrol craft needed for harbor protection,
and he stressed the extreme need for escort. He wrote: "We
must get every ship that sails the seas under constant close
protection." But he understood fully the magnitude of that
job. He ended his memorandum:

> "It is not easy to create an adequate and compre-
> hensive escort system. Our coastal sea lanes, in which
> I include the Caribbean and Panama routes, total 7,000
> miles in length. To this must be added the ocean con-
> voy system to Great Britain and Iceland (which is al-
> ready in effect) and extensions which should be made
> to protect traffic to the east coast of South America
> (and perhaps to the Cape of Good Hope), not to
> mention our Pacific Ocean commitments.
> "An enormous number of seagoing vessels is re-

ANOTHER SURVIVOR. An aerial photograph of a tanker torpedoed off the Atlantic Coast during the worst phase of the Battle of the Atlantic. Her crew stayed with her although men were killed and injured. They controlled the fire and finally extinguished it. Then the vessel was towed into port by the United States Navy, repaired, and sent back to sea again.

quired, as well as very large air forces. Aviation for ocean coverage must be taken along in auxiliary carriers. For convoys moving close to land the air should operate from shore bases. While observation planes can be used for certain limited missions, the bulk of the shore-based aviation should be of the patrol or medium bomber type. Land types are essential in freezing

AND ANOTHER. The American tanker *E. H. Blum* broke in half after being torpedoed off the Atlantic Coast. Her stern rested on the bottom in shallow water. The sections were towed in separately to Newport News, Virginia. They were joined together in the shipyard, and, triumphantly, *E. H. Blum* returned to service.

LIBERTY SHIP THAT WOULDN'T SINK. Struck hard aft by a torpedo, this vessel kept alive, maintained herself afloat for seventy-two hours, and reached port.

weather because sea planes ice up on the water. All planes must have radar. All must have crews specially trained in the technique of anti-submarine operations and must be able to operate at night as well as by day."

Patrol craft were assembled and based throughout the West Indian islands, and a convoy system was established as far south as Panama. But Doenitz, as the pressure against him was increased, withdrew his U-boats from the region. The swaggering young Nazis with their shoulder-long hair and heavy, black leather sea boots had become quite familiar to the natives in certain parts of the Caribbean. They had swum from coral beaches, and bartered for rum and turtle meat, or, with the consent of their officers, painted heraldic designs on the conning towers. These had been noticed by survivors, and among the more fanciful were dragons, goats' heads, unicorns, and mailed gauntlets.

Their new orders sent them thousands of miles from the Caribbean to the bleak, ice-rimmed route past the North Cape of Norway into the Russian ports of Murmansk and Archangel. In the Caribbean the hurricane season was about to begin, and would divert or reduce shipping. Up off the North Cape, though, large Allied convoys sailed from Iceland during the period of twenty-four hour daylight. Doenitz had taken three million tons of shipping while *Paukenschlag* had lasted. He was content to leave the Western Hemisphere to a few of his long-range craft and find new targets for his fleet.

CONVOY was not the answer to the U-boat problem. That was the bitter realization made by the United States and British navies at the end of the first year of joint operation in the war. The only real way to meet Doenitz's threat was by the destruction of his bases along the French coast, where in the huge, concrete-slab pens the underwater craft were equipped, repaired, and made ready for sea almost without interruption. The nightly Royal Air Force raids against them failed to have any severe effect, and the U-boats went to sea just about when they wished.

Meanwhile, the strain remained savagely hard on the men of the American and British merchant marines. The

British already had a huge casualty list from the 1939-41 period, when they had served practically alone. And in Washington a record kept by the War Shipping Administration showed that American personnel losses in the opening six months of the war were greater than those suffered during the entire course of World War I.

The American and British navies, aided by the Canadian Navy and the Free French and Free Polish naval forces, tried their utmost to furnish sufficient escort for the vitally important transatlantic convoys. It was not their fault that the ghastly toll of men and ships lost kept mounting week after week. Then, finally, in the spring of 1943, there were enough escort vessels, sufficient armament and trained crews to check the U-boats.

The early transatlantic convoys had, though, achieved their purpose. Without their arrival in the Allied ports overseas, the war would certainly have gone to the Axis. Escort-guarded convoy in great part had proved itself. The Allies expanded the system, improved upon it, introduced new types of escort vessels and antisubmarine devices and weapons. There were by 1943 convoys that sailed into every theater of operation and across all of the major oceans of the world.

Convoy was of course a number of things. It had been used variously by the British, the French, the Dutch, and the Spanish ever since the time of piracy. During World War I, the British had employed the escort-guarded convoy method with considerable success, and in 1917-18 the United States Navy took a very active share in North Atlantic escort duty.

Organization of the World War II convoys, particularly

those designated for the Atlantic traverse, was very complicated. Plans for a sailing were made weeks and sometimes
months in advance. The last step before a convoy shoved off,
either from an American port or homeward bound from
overseas, was a conference attended by the shipmasters
whose vessels were assigned to it.

They met in the office of the port director and discussed
with the convoy commodore, usually a veteran naval
officer, the route to be taken, the U-boat dangers, the possible enemy surface and aircraft power, the weather and sea
conditions to be encountered. Each shipmaster was issued
definite, separate, and secret instructions and a secret code
book for the flag and other types of signal communications
—whistle blasts, lights, and rockets—to be used during the
voyage. Each ship was given a number in the convoy, and a
station therein, with orders to keep that station unless commanded otherwise at sea.

The secret orders were issued in long brown envelopes,
and masters hurried to open them once the conference was
over and they were back aboard their ships. Then they
called their chief officers and navigators into the chart-
rooms. The required courses were laid off, and the procedure checked for emergency turns and evasive tactics. The
bulky Mersigs book that carried the signal codes was
studied, and the time-zone changes that would be in force
at sea. The captain talked with the Armed Guard officer,
discussing with him his duties.

The chart drawer was locked afterward, and so was the
chartroom itself until sailing hour. The master took with
him to his own quarters the batch of orders. He put them
in a special weighted bag that he kept ready to pitch into

the sea in case of disaster. When that was done, he stretched out for the last untroubled sleep he would have for some nights to come.

Convoy was made up as soon as the ships were outside the mine-gate of the port of departure. Navy signalmen handled the numbers pennants flying from the bridge halyards as the ships maneuvered into column and station order. The commodore's ship, as well as those of the vice- and rear commodore and of the column leaders, and the signal-repeating and rescue ships, had been designated at the shore conference. Within an hour or so, depending upon the size of the convoy and the weather and sea conditions, departure was made.

Overhead, if the convoy was leaving the States, were Coast Guard and Navy and Army and Civil Air Patrol planes, and slow, low-flying Navy blimps. Aboard the merchant ships, the Armed Guard detachments stood by their weapons, closely watched by their officers. Some of Doenitz's most effective attacks had been delivered right outside a mine-gate.

The convoy was a number, a colored pin upon an immense wall chart in naval headquarters in Washington, London, and Ottawa. Tremendous effort had gone into the gathering of the ships, then the recruitment of their crews, and the loading, the fueling and victualing, and the stowage of explosive cargo and ammunition. But, there was a further form of extraordinary activity connected with the sailing of a convoy. This was the operation of the intricate, carefully planned network of escort rendezvous points, courses and alternate courses, and straggler routes. Added to it as a constantly changing factor was the disposition of

Doenitz's underwater force while the Germans sought to find a vulnerable point for attack.

The United States Navy had been occupied with North Atlantic escort duty as early as 1941, when Admiral Ernest J. King, the commander in chief, had issued on November 17 his revised Escort-of-Convoy Instructions. Admiral King ordered that "the guiding principle shall be that, whenever it is possible, escorts will be so disposed that no submarine can reach a successful firing position without being detected." The escort vessels were to "patrol their assigned areas as far as may be practicable."

Admiral King advised that zigzag courses be used for fast convoys, and for the small convoy with a narrow front. He pointed out that it was necessary for large or slow convoys to maintain a straight course. For them, zigzagging reduced the distance made good, caused confusion and straggling, and had not proven effective in avoiding submarines. Evasive courses, which meant changes of 20 degrees to 50 degrees on each side of the base course, held for periods of two to six hours, were the recommended alternative for large, slow convoys.

The usual convoy formation spread ships out over a considerable area. A distance of a thousand feet was supposed to be kept between vessels in column, and a space of six hundred feet between columns. None of the merchant ships had radar, and only a very few of the big troop transports were equipped with the asdic sonar device. Keeping station was often a nerve-shattering experience for the convoy watch officers. "Fast" convoys in the first year of the war were supposed to hold a speed of 9 knots. "Slow" convoys wobbled along at 6.5 knots and sometimes below that, while their escorts wound around and around and around, aware that they presented a perfect target for any of Doenitz's sharpshooters.

Blackout in a convoy was complete at night. Orders were strictly enforced; a ship that showed a light was to be fired upon by machine guns without warning. But emergency turns were practiced, the orders transmitted by combinations of varicolored lights displayed from "Christmas trees," steel-pole structures reared above the wheelhouse topsides. These were quite regularly read wrong by part of the convoy, and ship slammed into ship in the darkness—some of them tankers full of high-test gasoline, some loaded with hundreds of tons of TNT, and others troop transports. The escort vessels, simply to stay alive, took off until the melee was over and the commodore called for a return to stations.

During daylight hours, more sense was made out of flag hoists and whistle signals, although in heavy weather they could be readily garbled. Fog buoys, cruciform-shaped spars painted white and hauled from a painter at the stern of each merchant ship in convoy, were designed to be an aid in keeping station at night. As they were dragged over the surface of the sea the buoys were supposed to kick up wakes visible to the lookouts and watch officers of the ships astern. But these were often lost as the painters broke or the vessels astern ran them down in near-misses.

There were many incidents where ships were severely hurt in convoy. No official figure was ever released, but destroyers were sorely rammed, one cut in half in collision. The total damage done by Allied ships to their column neighbors and the escorts surpassed the losses suffered in enemy action.

It was understandable. Ships were ordered to keep station during fog or during snow gales in freezing weather. With their steerageway greatly reduced, and with ice sheathing their sides as well as the huge heaps of deck cargo and covering the superstructures and masts as high as the crosstrees platforms, vessels lurched along an approximation of the base course. Communication could only be maintained with the commodore's ship or any other ship through use of the TBY, a small, portable voice radio. But interference was frequent, and messages readily garbled or heard only in part. Whistle blasts were used as warning: first the column number, blatted out into the wind shriek, then the ship's number, and as other vessels replied, the signal was repeated, and the convoy proceeded by that guidance alone.

With dawn, damage was inspected, and the sorely hurt left the convoy in charge of an escort vessel for the nearest friendly port. The commodore had a great deal to say over the TBY about station keeping, and flag hoists were repeated down the newly reformed columns; stragglers appeared in custody of a destroyer or a corvette to the accompaniment of strongly worded advice delivered through a bullhorn on the warship's bridge.

There were a few merchant-ship captains who, by their own private admission, were willing to meet all the risks the enemy offered and make the voyage unescorted. They purposely dropped out of their convoy soon after it was formed, took to the straggler routes, and often arrived in the ports overseas days ahead of the convoy to which they had been attached. Boasting entered their talk, and bitterness. They had taken enough, they said, of Navy discipline; they were tired of the commodore's talks at dusk over the TBY about stragglers, station keeping, excessive

FLAGS STILL FLYING. The strategic breakwater of beached ships, called Operation Mulberry, is put in place June, 1944, as a key part of the Normandy beachhead. There are twenty-three ships in this section of the line. Most of them are American freighters and tankers, and alongside them are Navy landing craft. They give protection to the improvised piers used for emergency cargo handling that are built between them and the beach.

stack smoke, and the right time to blow furnace tubes. A war could be fought in two ways, and this was one of them.

But the convoy system, despite obvious faults, remained the principal protective measure against the enemy. It was only under extremely heavy enemy attack or violent weather conditions that the formations could not be held. Then casualties inevitably occurred. Doenitz could report a new list of sinkings to Hitler. A few survivors taken aboard the rescue ships were brought into port, their hands and feet frostbitten and about to become gangrenous.

The technical side of North Atlantic convoy duty was

STORM WRECKS MULBERRY. The Germans could not figure out Mulberry in time to stop its construction. But a violent storm that rose soon after D-day created enormous damage. A Coast Guard combat photographer took this picture while a huge wave was whipping over *Centurion*, the principal link in the chain of sunken ships that formed the breakwater. The structure was repaired when the storm passed and was again used for the unloading of supplies vitally needed by the combat units inland.

often overlooked or not clearly understood by the majority of the men in the merchant-ship crews. They were too busy with their own duties and were also repelled by the Navy insistence upon complicated symbolism, strange names, strings of numbers and letters, and code secrecy. Still, veteran seamen were forced to admit that "gold braid and all," the Navy was doing a good job.

The Navy convoy system really involved a formidable set of terms that multiplied as the war continued. It started with OPNAV, which meant the Chief of Naval Operations at Washington. OPNAV was in charge of all convoy routing.

It designated four or more ocean positions, each given 'a letter-combination symbol through which the convoy was ordered to sail. A MOMP, a mid-ocean meeting point, was established south of Newfoundland and called WESTOMP, and another, EASTOMP, approximately five hundred miles off Northern Ireland.

When OPNAV had fully approved the route, usually eight days before the convoy sailing date, it was transmitted to the British Admiralty and to the Commander in Chief Atlantic Fleet, who was known as CINCLANT, to the British Commander in Chief of the Western Approaches, CINCWA, to the commander of the task force that supplied the escort, to the British Commanding Officer Atlantic Coast, COAC, whose headquarters were at Halifax, and to Canadian Naval Staff Headquarters, NSHQ, at Ottawa, and to the Flag Officer Newfoundland Forces, FONF, at St. John's, and to the Canadian port director concerned, who had no code name.

The old-time merchant-shipmasters shook their heads when presented with orders that contained these and other seemingly fanciful terms. They knew, vaguely, that a "sea approach" was supposed to extend two hundred miles from a coast, but as for the rest of it, that was completely strange. And how was a man to pronounce NSHQ?

There was little that the independent-minded shipmasters could do in rejection of this system. The one obvious trick was to become a straggler, peel off from convoy formation as soon as possible. But most masters refused to accept this as a sensible way out of their troubles and sailed in convoy. They were proven right, and after 1942 very few American masters left the escort-guarded formations to make the voyage on their own.

Ships that had loaded at Baltimore or Philadelphia made all possible speed to reach New York with whatever coastal escort and air cover was available, then laid over for a night in New York. They were joined there by the ships that were locally loaded, and at dawn proceeded up the East River into Long Island Sound and through the Cape Cod Canal, using every possible bit of protection before the final solitary dash was started for Halifax.

Back in Bedford Basin, the almost completely land-locked rear harbor of the Nova Scotian port, the ships waited at anchor until a convoy formed. United States Navy escort vessels picked up the convoys at WESTOMP, taking over from the Canadian Navy units that operated out of Halifax and St. Johns. The system looked good on paper, and the ship movements seemed to go smoothly enough across the charts in the various Allied headquarters.

But there were all sorts of complications at sea. The Navy's main pursuit instrument was asdic (the name is an abbreviation for Anti-Submarine Detection Investigation Committee), a device that was supposed to discover enemy underwater craft by sonic contact. There was no doubt that many asdic "bounce-backs" located German submarines; still, a great number of depth charges were also dumped on whales, schools of fish, and, in shallow waters, on submerged wrecks. German submarine crews were also adept at making short turns which induced the asdic operator to take the U-boat's wake for the vessel herself and drop the depth charges wide of the target.

Life aboard the escort vessels was not easy. Radio communication was often poor, with equipment lacking or in bad shape or manned by untrained personnel. Full operational use of the SG radar was not yet familiar to men who only a few months before had been civilians. Gunnery was another partial mystery, along with the setting of depth-charge patterns. So escort crews kept contact with their convoy charges by signal hoists, whistle blasts, a sparing display of the "Christmas tree" lights, the TBY radio, and in great emergency voice messages passed ship to ship by bullhorn.

Winter weather on the North Atlantic offered extreme handicaps for the maintenance of convoy formation. A miserable Christmas at sea was passed by Convoy HX-166 in the first month of the war. It had left Halifax thirty-six vessels strong, but only six met the escort at WESTOMP. The United States Navy escort commander was persistent; he cruised around the meeting place for more than twenty-four hours and, with the aid of an observation plane, picked up twenty-two other ships, including the commodore's vessel. But time could not be spared to find the eight still missing, and they made the voyage by themselves. The masters of the ships that had sailed independently later expressed considerable satisfaction. Due to bad weather, MOMP had been changed three times for the convoy, and some of the escort vessels were forced to pull out of the screen and head for Iceland because of fuel shortage.

During the early months of the war, though, Doenitz's craft were almost completely occupied further south, along the American coast. The usual escort force of two destroyers and four corvettes was able to keep the North Atlantic convoys reasonably intact until they reached port. The only convoy that lost heavily during that period was

ON-67, made up of thirty-five ships that sailed in eight columns. It had the bad luck to be sent westward in February at the time of a full moon.

The ocean escort for it was made up of United States Navy destroyers, *Edison, Lea, Nicholson,* and *Bernadou,* under Commander A. C. Murdaugh. They steamed south from Iceland and met the convoy about twenty-four hours after the time set for rendezvous. *Nicholson* was the only warship with her radar in working condition, so the Canadian Navy ship *Algona,* which had been part of the British escort, stayed with the convoy. Another British ship, the specially designed rescue vessel S.S. *Toward,* was called upon to use her high frequency radio direction finder for enemy detection.

Toward caught a submarine signal at 5:30 P.M., or 1730 in the Navy fashion, on February 21, 1942, and *Lea* steamed out along the bearing in search. No contact was made; *Lea* returned to the convoy and resumed station. But at 0305 the next morning, two ships of the convoy were torpedoed and sunk. Sweeps were made by the destroyers during February 22 and February 23 without any result. Then in the bleak hours before dawn on February 24, four merchant ships were struck.

There was plenty of work for *Toward,* with her big rescue net rigged outboard on a cargo boom, her whaleboat crew which fished survivors from the water, and her Royal Navy surgeon, who tended to them in the sick bay. A rocket known as a "snowflake" had been fired from a projector to illuminate the scene of disaster. The brightly burning powder showed no signs of U-boats though—only the wounded and those already dead.

Toward again reported suspicious signals picked up on her direction finder during the morning watch. Commander Murdaugh sent out *Nicholson* and *Lea* to investigate, and the destroyers reported sighting a pair of U-boats cruising on the surface near the convoy. But before he could make a radical course change or disperse the ships, he had to get consent from Washington. Commander Murdaugh waited almost seven hours after his radio message was dispatched before approval came from Washington. Then darkness had come down over the sullen, misty sea and the moon had not yet risen.

The convoy shuffled around through a 68-degree course change, and soon afterward U-boat contact was made. Depth charges were dropped while the destroyers steadily patrolled. No direct hits were made, but the submarines did not return to the attack. ON-67 came safely into port with her survivors.

During the next few months and on into the summer of 1942, when Doenitz mounted a series of almost irresistible attacks, the convoy system improved. Convoy commanders could take evasive action in extreme circumstances without Washington's prior approval. The United States Navy continued to keep general strategic control over the western half of the Atlantic, and the Royal Navy held absolute control over the eastern half. Air coverage was gradually extended until Allied planes could patrol an area that reached four hundred miles east of Newfoundland, five hundred miles south of Iceland, and seven hundred miles west of the British Isles. But this left the big mid-ocean area north of the Azores unprotected, and it became a favorite hunting ground for U-boats. Air bases in the Azores were established in 1943, but by then Doenitz had sunk many ships with his newly formed and powerful wolf-pack formations.

The wolf packs contained the largest, fastest, and most effective U-boats, which hunted Allied shipping eight and ten together. Doenitz stationed them along all of the main transatlantic routes that convoys might use and unified them by radio contact with scout submarines that cruised around the Allied rendezvous points already known to the Germans.

The wolf packs earned their name. They attacked every transatlantic merchant convoy during August, 1942. The score of sinkings climbed alarmingly high again: eighty-eight ships that aggregated 454,548 tons in September. Convoy escorts fought back with all they had, but it was not enough. The wolf packs continued to kill. Convoy SC-104 lost eight ships in two night attacks south of Cape Farewell, and HX-212 lost five in four attacks that went on day after day. The October toll for the northern route surpassed the rest: twenty-seven ships with a tonnage of nearly 189,000 were lost.

But that was not the worst. The figures for November cited a loss of over 600,000 tons of shipping in the Atlantic. Then, in January, 1943, in a fight where the wolf-pack members outnumbered the escorts two to one, there were seven Allied tankers sunk. It was the highest percentage of loss by enemy submarine action during the war; the original convoy had numbered only nine vessels.

Wolf packs roaming the convoy routes in February and March, the months of bitter gales, freezing weather, and poor visibility, kept their score high. They accounted for

THE BRITISH HAVE BETTER LUCK. The British prefabricated harbor on the Normandy coast, built with a concrete caisson breakwater, held together in the stormy weather of June, 1944. Liberty ships are at the moorings in the foreground inside the breakwater. The farthest pier at the left is for barges. The piers in the center are for ship use. The shorter pier at the right is for LST's (landing ships big enough to carry tanks).

thirty-six ships of 227,109 tons in February, and in March they sank eighty-five ships, of more than 500,000 tons aggregate.

Doenitz had been made Commander in Chief of the German Navy by Hitler. He moved his headquarters to Berlin in an aura of great hope, although there were other high-ranking Nazi officers who thought the war was lost. Doenitz's assurance of victory came from the tremendous number of U-boat sinkings. January and March gave him the greatest scores; he wrote after the war, "The number of U-boats was constantly increasing, losses were slight."

His feeder submarines, the "milch cows," were at sea to bring fuel, spare parts, and fresh ammunition to the patrol craft. British bombings still had done very little harm to the U-boat pens on the French coast. The new acoustical torpedo was nearly ready to be used as was the *schnorchel* breathing device. Doenitz could also report to Hitler that a few tankers had sneaked past the Allied blockade formations and reached the South Atlantic and the Indian Ocean to refuel and resupply the U-boats there.

American merchant seamen were aware of these facts in a general way. Their sources of information were extremely limited. Even while ashore, their great preoccupation was survival. They thought, talked, dreamed of little else. The threat of death dominated their lives, especially during that 1942-43 winter.

Most torpedoed men never had a chance once they were in the water. They were rendered numb at contact with it; the average temperature was about 30 degrees Fahrenheit. They began to freeze before they could shout or move much. They died hunched turtlelike in their life jackets, a patina of ice upon them. Those who managed to get away in lifeboats or on rafts had somewhat better luck. But exposure killed many of them, and nearly all were in bad shape when picked up by rescue vessels.

Captain F. C. Denebrink, USN, in command of the hard-worked cruiser U.S.S. *Brooklyn*, realized the paramount importance of rescue tactics and made an intensive study of the problem. *Brooklyn* took part on September 3, 1942, in a spectacular operation in which she saved 1,173 people from the troop transport *Wakefield*, which had caught fire at sea. But it was performed in fair weather and during daylight with a destroyer to guard *Brooklyn* and the other rescue vessel, the destroyer *Mayo*, from submarine attack.

There were very few mass rescues as Doenitz intensified his attack and fought to control the North Atlantic with his new, powerful craft. Fast passenger liners that possessed the speed of *Queen Mary* and *Queen Elizabeth*, *Empress of Scotland* and *Pasteur*, were able to run alone as transports and keep out of the way of the U-boats. The smaller, slower ships received the battering, and no amount of skillful rescue work could save their crews from eventual destruction. The 1942-43 winter was a dread, awful period for the men of the American merchant marine.

The losses suffered by the Greenland-bound convoy SG-19 made one of the most tragic stories of the war. The little, miserably equipped formation—two merchant ships and the 5,252-ton Army transport *Dorchester*—left St. John's, Newfoundland, for Skovford on January 29, 1943, in foul weather. *Dorchester* was the principal vessel to be guarded; she carried 751 passengers, most of them troops, a

THERE ARE THE SHIPS. This is the English Channel
during the Allied conquest of the Cherbourg Peninsula.
So many vessels have gathered that they form an almost
solid mass offshore. LST's and other landing craft shuttle
ceaselessly back and forth between the ships and the
beach. Troops are sent off in motorized columns toward
the front and with them ammunition and gasoline. Those
are barrage balloons over the beach, supposed to keep
low-flying Nazi planes away from the shipping.

merchant crew of 130 men, and 23 men in her Armed
Guard detachment.

Escort was given by a Coast Guard unit, three cutters
whose best speed was 11.5 knots, considerably less than
necessary to be effective against U-boats. They were *Comanche, Tampa,* and *Escanaba,* their depth charges and
firing gear so thickly coated with ice as to be useless. From
time to time, during the gale that swept the convoy, they

were forced to heave to, while live steam was used to remove topside ice which would soon capsize them.

Escanaba guarded *Dorchester* on the starboard side, but *Escanaba's* radar was not working. U-boat 456 put a torpedo into *Dorchester* at 0355, in total darkness, on February 3, and the transport's people had no warning at all.

There was not even enough steam left to blow the six whistle blasts of the abandon-ship signal. Lack of power kept the radio silent. No man aboard *Dorchester* thought of sending up rockets or flares. The escort kept steaming ahead on course until after the transport sank by the bow.

She was equipped with fourteen lifeboats. Only two of them were successfully launched. Her rafts were released before headway was lost; they drifted astern, most of them empty. The water temperature was 36 degrees Fahrenheit. Men who jumped over the side did not last long. Those who were saved were in almost every case hauled loglike from the sea by Coast Guardsmen who dived in for them from the cutters *Escanaba* and *Comanche*. Other Coast Guardsmen swam out to life rafts loaded with numbed, half-dead survivors, and rowed or paddled back to the ships through the darkness and the gale.

Many of the soldiers went down with the ship, among them the four chaplains of various faiths who had given their life belts to others. It was reported later that the chaplains stood side by side, quietly, in the final moment.

The full complement aboard *Dorchester* was 904 men. Of these, 299 were saved.

News of her sinking came as an enormous shock to the American public. It was a jolting, almost frightening reminder of what happened at sea. But neither the American nor the British people were informed of the severity of the March, 1943, sinkings. Doenitz's wolf packs, spread across the North Atlantic and in close communication with one another, destroyed forty-one ships in the first ten days of that month. Then, in the next ten days of March, they took care of forty-four more. A total of more than 500,000 tons of shipping was lost within twenty days.

Doenitz operated daily an average of 116 submarines in the North Atlantic. There was no possibility of routing convoys beyond their reach. Evasive courses steered from one wolf pack meant discovery by another. The entire convoy system was about to disintegrate; 68 per cent of the escort forces were injured and kept in shipyards for repair. What was left of convoys came into port with six, eight, ten, and twelve ships missing.

Crews were found. New convoys were formed and sent to sea. Escort ships returned for duty and busily engaged the enemy. Losses were cut in the last few days of March; by April, they had been reduced a great deal. The Battle of the Atlantic had turned toward the Allies.

But the American public had not yet been fully informed of the losses suffered on the Murmansk run in the early phases of the war. Accounts that told of those convoys were just becoming known. Survivors had begun to arrive by the hundreds with the ships that were left. The United States Navy released some information. The War Shipping Administration gave out a few more medals. The Royal Navy commended a convoy for its behavior in battle. There, between Iceland and North Russia, another fierce and tragically costly sea campaign was still to be decided.

CARGO for North Russia was hauled from American ports over a distance of more than 5,000 miles. Most of the loading was done in Philadelphia and New York, and in the fateful year of 1942 the ships generally ran alone to Halifax, the make-up point for the first of several convoys they would join. The ships carried clothing, and medical supplies, and powdered eggs and milk, but their main cargo was ammunition and cased TNT, tanks and planes.

The ships were deeply loaded, often with a dangerously low freeboard. Tanks and planes were stowed on deck, lashed to ringbolts with steel wire to keep them from going overside in a storm. Plank catwalks for the use of the crew were constructed over the deck cargo, narrow and difficult to maneuver at night or in battle.

Murmansk-bound convoys bore the designation PQ and were numbered. When the return voyage was made, the designation was reversed and became QP, according to Royal Navy procedure adopted early in the war. The typical convoy leaving Halifax consisted of thirty-three merchant ships and as many as ten escort vessels if they were available. Spread out in column formation, it stretched over an area four nautical miles wide, and a mile and a half from the first to the last row of ships. Lean, gray-hulled American destroyers and Coast Guard cutters guarded the ships, along with the chunkier, camouflage-mottled Canadian and British corvettes. In addition to these there were, when they could be put into service, the new United States Navy destroyer escorts, a smaller version of the standard destroyer, and British beam trawlers converted for convoy work, and the specially equipped Royal Navy rescue ships.

Convoy speed was eight knots or less. Station keeping was difficult in fog, snow, and total blackout. Ships fell astern, became stragglers, and before the escort could bring them back were caught and sunk by U-boats. Almost every night during the blackout hours there was some sort of collision in column, and vessels known as "rompers" steamed far ahead of the convoy much to the anger of the escort commander and the commodore.

But despite their losses, their mistakes, and the lack of naval discipline, the convoys reached port in either Iceland or Scotland. Ships were sent into the Scottish ports to be armed and to take aboard ammunition. They lay in the Clyde, at the Tail o' the Bank, off gray granite Gourock

and Greenock, while they were fitted with light-caliber machine guns of World War I manufacture, then were sent
north to Loch Ewe or Loch Gare, where they received their
ammunition.

They stood out afterward from the western Scottish
coast on the course for Iceland. Royal Air Force planes
were overhead, and some of the escort towed observation
balloons aloft on cables. The U-boats would still be a great
threat on the run from Iceland to North Russia, the merchant crews knew. But they would also meet the *Luftwaffe*,
be bombed and strafed by veteran German pilots. Men
took the canvas covers from the machine guns, examined
the weapons again, tried the action, swung them at imag-
inary targets. They would need these, and soon.

Iceland was snow-covered mountains where volcanoes
steamed and shaggy ponies ran over chocolate-colored tun-
dra. The harbors of Reykjavik and Hvalfjordur held
hundreds of ships. This was the make-up point for the final
leg of the Murmansk haul, two thousand miles up around
Bear Island and then southward, skirting the ice fields, into
the Kola Inlet. Some ships had orders that took them to
Archangel, two days' steaming further to the east and
south, but for most of the run the convoy would sail as a
single formation.

The area to be feared the most was off the North Cape
of Norway. There, German planes would be flying from
nearby bases, making repeated attacks. U-boats would be
with them, sailing from captured ports in Norway and Fin-
land. Hitler took a personal hand in this; he wanted to
crush absolutely any attempt to bring help to the Russians.
And he held his prize warships in Norwegian fjords, ready

to go out against the Royal Navy if it showed itself in sufficient force as convoy escort.

North Russian convoys left Iceland by way of the Denmark Strait, standing clear of huge mine fields and often in frozen fog that drifted wraithlike over the lead gray sea. With luck, and without too much German opposition, the crews could hope to be in North Russia at the end of ten days. But there was no night during the summer months in these latitudes, and Doenitz had his scout craft in a gantlet that extended from the North Cape to the polar icecap past Bear Island. Big German patrol planes, Focke-Wulf Condors that the Allied seamen came to call "the vultures," ranged over the same region and reported at once when contact had been made with the enemy.

Convoy PQ-13 was picked up on March 28 while it labored through a heavy gale off the Norwegian coast. Submarines guided by the patrol planes ranged alongside and began to fire their torpedoes. The escort cruiser H.M.S. *Trinidad* was struck, and the destroyer *Eclipse*, and a merchant ship in the outboard, starboard column. Then the commodore's ship took a torpedo in her afterhold, where she carried land mines. She was gone in forty seconds, leaving only a few survivors in the freezing water.

Stragglers from PQ-13 made their way into Murmansk singly for several days after the escort force was broken. They were very lucky; the gale persisted and gave them cover, and Doenitz and the *Luftwaffe* commander later sent their units to meet the new Murmansk-bound convoy PQ-15 off the North Cape.

A Focke-Wulf patrol plane had sighted PQ-15 when the ships were three days out of Iceland. Among them were the

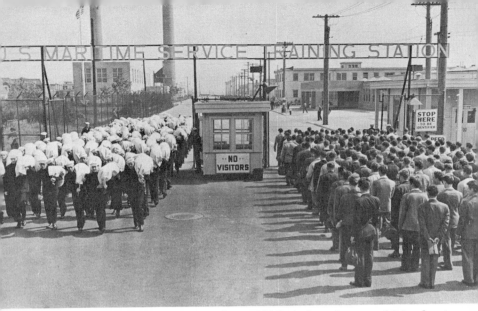

THE YOUNG HOPEFULS. A detachment of Merchant Marine apprentice seamen trained at Sheepshead Bay, New York City, marches out while a fresh lot stands by to enter. More than 250,000 men received Maritime Service instruction during the war. The Sheepshead Bay station was the largest of its kind in the world.

American freighters *Expositor, Lancaster, Zebulon B. Vance, Paul Luckenbach,* and *Alcoa Rambler.* They were under combined air and submarine attack that began May 2 and lasted for more than forty-eight hours.

Snow flurries obscured the enemy for part of the time. The low-flying Heinkel torpedo bombers were able to come in low, right above the mast tops, and whip down the columns for the ship picked as target. Then a wing tip tilted, and the torpedo beneath it was released. There was very little time for the merchant-ship gunners to halt the attack.

The commodore's ship was sunk, and another British freighter, and a Royal Navy corvette. *Cape Corso* was next; she was a big British freighter whose cargo was cordite. *Ex-*

positor was right alongside of her in column formation, and the American ship's cargo was ten thousand rounds of 75-millimeter and 37-millimeter shells, and five thousand cases of TNT.

Captain Julius Christoph Klepper rested motionless, without speech, in *Expositor's* bridge wing. He had seen the white-splattered passage of the Heinkel torpedo over the dark sea, the final upward skip at the instant of impact. *Cape Corso* was hit in Number Four hold.

There was no loud sound, just a deep, thick rumbling choked by the sea. But the blast knocked men backward on the decks of *Expositor*. Captain Klepper, hanging onto his bridge rail, looked over at the Number Four hatch on the British ship. It glared with a weird, almost blinding incandescence. A wind of destruction rose from *Cape Corso* and sucked flame the length of the ship. She sank stern first, her bow fiery.

The ship behind her in column was *Zebulon B. Vance.* Helm orders were given quickly by Captain Guy Hudgins, and the American ship steered clear. But the men from *Cape Corso* were all dead. Their bodies jerked with the turbulence of the sea; their eyes shone only because shock had flipped on the little battery-fed light bulbs on the collars of their life jackets.

German attack still continued, and the gun crews aboard both *Expositor* and *Vance* were shorthanded. They were forced to fire as fast as the guns could be worked, merchant-seamen volunteers serving alongside the Armed Guard. It was after they had reached Murmansk in a snow gale on May 5 and lay anchored, ready to discharge cargo, that they talked about *Cape Corso.* Some men's hands twitched as they spoke of her; others had been partially deafened by battle and shouted; there were among the rest several who did nothing but mumble.

Convoy PQ-16 formed for Murmansk and Archangel and left Iceland on May 20 protected by very strong escort. It was now the season of the year for daylight to last throughout all twenty-four hours. The Germans were aware of this and had prepared for it. Spies reported that at the Norwegian bases the *Luftwaffe* squadrons had been greatly increased and Doenitz's flotillas reinforced.

Thirty-four merchant ships were in PQ-16 when it stood northward into the Denmark Strait accompanied by two Royal Navy cruisers of the *Dorsetshire* class, two of the *Southampton* class, two flak (antiaircraft) ships, six destroyers, six armed trawlers, and two submarines. But many of the merchant ships were armed with no more than light-caliber machine guns, .30 Hotchkisses and Marlins. And several ships were without armament of any sort.

Five days out of Iceland, the running battle started. It was to last steadily for six days until the survivors of the convoy fought their way into the Kola Inlet to Murmansk or continued on to Archangel. Magnetic mines and huge contact mines lowered by parachute from German bombers strewed the sea. Icebergs drifted across the convoy course, pale, lovely, and immense; tall Polar bears crouched in terror along their ridges.

U-boats circled the convoy, waiting for the moment. The sea, the air, constantly shivered with the concussion of mines, depth charges, torpedoes, shells, bombs, and exploding ships. Sirens screamed warning aboard destroyers as they swept up and down the ship columns and dropped depth charges to detonate German mines or aerial and underwater torpedoes. Vast oil slicks covered the surface of the sea. Dead men clung frozen to pieces of flotsam. Overhead, the German planes passed across the often bright-blue and unclouded sky. They were rocked by black, jagged shell bursts, dived through skeins of tracers, their leading wing edges alight with machine-gun fire.

But on May 26 the four big cruisers were given orders to pull out of the escort. They could not be spared. There were still Hitler's pocket battleships in the Norwegian fjords to be fought. Merchant ships in the outboard columns, slow, clumsy, with engine and rudder trouble, were cruelly pounded by the Junker 88's, the Messerschmitt 110's, and the swift-diving Stukas, and the Heinkels.

Ammunition was exhausted during the almost incessant battle action the next day. The old American freighter *Mauna Kea* made a signal to the new Liberty ship *John Randolph* that she had none left. The Armed Guard officer aboard *Randolph* talked with the master of the ship, and permission was granted. A hatch was opened, cargo broached, and *Mauna Kea* supplied with the badly needed rounds for her guns.

It was reckoned that the *Luftwaffe* had put 125 planes into the air. They came low over the columns, careless of the weak defensive fire. The commodore's ship, *Ocean Voice*, carried a Spitfire plane on her foredeck. That was launched by catapult, and the young RAF sergeant pilot took her straight up against the Germans. He shot down two bombers before he was caught in *Luftwaffe* cross fire. But he parachuted out and was picked up from the sea by a corvette.

Ocean Voice was immediately made a major target and took a bomb on her foredeck. She was temporarily disabled, and some of her people wounded. The commodore transferred his flag to one of the antiaircraft ships; the German pilots turned away for easier game.

The Russian freighter *Staraya Bolshevik* was strafed and bombed in the center of the convoy. A bomb hit her forward, crashed into the bosun's paint and stores lockers, and she was set afire. She was steered off the wind and lay without headway while the fire was fought. Most of her cargo was ammunition; the crew worked rapidly under the German strafing attacks. They were helped by a pair of corvettes which lay alongside her and lent their hoses and extinguishers and the protection of their guns.

Ocean Voice made repairs and came back on station. *Staraya Bolshevik*'s fire was put out, and she got under way again. The battle dragged through the fifth day and into the sixth. Gunners counted the rounds that remained to them. Defense could not last many hours longer.

But on the sixth day, steaming fast in the snow flurries which reached out from the dark, rugged coast, a flotilla of three Russian destroyers joined the convoy.

The Russians were excellent antiaircraft gunners. *Luftwaffe* pilots were soon discouraged and had lost a considerable part of their original force. The German planes disappeared. The convoy broke formation, and one small segment kept on toward Archangel. The rest of the ships moved in single file through the mine gate and into the Kola Inlet. For the first time in six days, the flag hoist AK1, meaning "Enemy aircraft coming," was taken from the halyards.

The ships were held for a month at Murmansk while cargo was discharged and a destroyer was sent to Scotland for ammunition for the return voyage. Murmansk, with its ten badly battered docks and railroad spurs, was a prime German target for the *Luftwaffe* just thirty-five miles away at the Finnish front. Sunken and beached ships littered the inlet. Gutted, blackened houses built of logs rested stark in the city among concrete-slab apartment houses and the squat, solid Arctica Hotel.

There was no relief from battle conditions. Gunners stood constant watch beside their pieces. Shore leave was no more than a couple of hours and a glass of strictly rationed vodka at the Seamen's Club. Then orders came to form convoy for home, and at the end of June the ships took column and started up into the Barents Sea.

The orders read to proceed as far north as possible within two hundred miles of the Pole past Bear Island. But the long-range German patrol planes found the convoy, reported its position. The bombers began to gather in the hazy sky, and the big black battle flag was flown on the commodore's halyards. Then, very suddenly, the *Luftwaffe* planes were gone. A strange silence came over the convoy.

It was broken by the clangor of battle to the south. That mounted and mounted and mounted, and the men in the homeward-bound convoy recognized with sharp pain what was happening beyond the horizon. A new convoy, PQ-17, bound for Murmansk out of Hvalfjordur, was under massive German attack.

For two days, while the homeward-bound ships steamed slowly south and west, their crews could hear sounds of the attacks made upon the PQ-17 convoy. They believed that the Allied ships suffered almost complete slaughter, and they were right.

Hitler had put into effect his plan of combined attack which the German Naval High Command called *Roessel-sprung*—"knight's gambit." He held the newly commissioned battleship *Tirpitz* at Trondheim with the heavy cruiser *Admiral Hipper*. Two more of his heavy cruisers, *Lutzow* and *Admiral Scheer*, were in Narvik waiting to be joined by another pair of their class, *Scharnhorst* and *Prinz Eugen*. A flotilla of a dozen destroyers was kept on stand-by to sail as the scout force.

Along a line that stretched from Jan Mayen Island, situated north of Iceland across any possible convoy route between it and the North Cape in Norway, the U-boats of the Northern Waters Flotilla were stationed. They were painted white with polar-bear symbols on their conning towers. Doenitz had increased the flotilla strength with U-boats brought by veteran commanders from the Atlantic Coast and the Caribbean. They kept close to the pack ice, cruising on the surface while they received reports of the convoy's progress by radio from the *Luftwaffe* patrol planes.

Orders were given for the *Luftwaffe* to keep two hundred planes in the air during the battle, and every other plane at the Norwegian and Finnish fields was held ready for replacement duty. It was impossible to conceal the movements of the convoy; German airmen and naval crews were informed of the departure within hours after PQ-17 left Iceland.

That was on June 28, and there were more escorts than merchant ships. The convoy went out in two divisions with an escort of six destroyers, four corvettes, seven trawlers, two submarines and two antiaircraft vessels. An additional covering force was given by the British Home Fleet and United States Navy units. Thirty-three merchant ships, twenty-two of them American, carried 18,000 tons of cargo, most of it explosives or high-test gasoline.

The two divisions closed into convoy formation when at sea and proceeded on a northerly course through thick fog and heavy ice floes. When they were about two hundred miles west of Bear Island on July 1 the first German reconnaissance planes were sighted, and they brought the U-boats. The next day, six U-boats attacked and were driven off by destroyers.

Course and speed were maintained. Snow, then fog, helped the convoy, but the Condor planes could be heard out on the horizon beyond gun range. The *Luftwaffe* began the battle on July 4 when twenty-six Heinkel torpedo bombers came in at fifty feet above the water, skipping along and across and over the columns. Stukas followed the Heinkels, dived plunging on the ships, their siren wails loud even in the clash of hundreds of guns.

Ships were being sunk. *Christopher Newport* and *William Hooper*, both new Liberties, were destroyed and with them a Russian tanker and two British freighters. The tanker flung a vast black smirch across the sky as she burned fore and aft. Heinkels climbed and reformed above it, came in again seven at a time, taking a single ship for their target.

But when their torpedoes were gone they withdrew. There was a lull. Men stood away from the guns in the convoy; wounded were tended; signals were passed from ship to ship. At 7:23 P.M., 1923 in the Navy fashion, the commodore signaled by firing a series of red and green Very lights. Their meaning was: "Scatter fanwise and proceed utmost speed."

The commodore was only obeying orders sent him by the British Admiralty. Those were: *Cruiser Force withdraw to westward at high speed. Owing to threat from surface ships, convoy is to disperse and proceed to Russian ports. Convoy is to scatter.* The Admiralty had been informed that Hitler's warships were out from the Norwegian bases and headed for the cruiser force.

It would be impossible for the Allied force to fight against the heavily armored German ships. But the Admiralty intelligence reports were faulty. The Germans had not yet left their bases. They did not leave them until the next day, July 5, when *Tirpitz, Scheer, Hipper,* seven destroyers, and three torpedo boats made a sortie off the North Cape. No Allied ships were found, and the Germans returned to port without a shot fired.

The merchant ships of PQ-17 were deserted by their escort though. They were left to scatter fanwise in a pitiful attempt to save themselves. They were already on the edge of the pack ice, could go no further northward. The dispersal point was 240 miles from the North Cape. They had to go more than 450 miles before they could find protection of any kind along the frozen, mountainous and uninhabited coast of Novaya Zemlya. That was to the east in Russian territory. They would be within easy range of the enemy while they tried to reach it.

The U-boats moved in, periscopes turning until the cross hairs were precisely on target. Ship after ship was sunk.

VICTORY ROW. The demands of the Pacific brought the Victory ship class into being. They were much faster than the Liberty and had the fuel capacity to make a round-trip Pacific run. Here a number of them are about to be completed in the fitting-out basin.

Luftwaffe pilots skirted low over the sea, hard to distinguish in the haze because of their silver or olive-green paint. They attacked ships singly and in formation, returned to make strafing runs with their machine guns after a bomb or a torpedo had struck aboard and the survivors tried to abandon.

The fury of the German attacks remained relentless. No mercy was shown. Some men aboard the Allied ships broke; their minds, their nerves, could not take this. Gunners kept on firing long after a German plane was gone. They screamed curses at the empty sky. Engine-rooms were deserted, and lookout stations. Men stood on deck with bowed heads, awaiting the end, mumbling. They wore their clumsy rubber suits that covered all parts of the body except the head and the hands. Those were supposed to help them in the freezing water, but they clutched cartons of cigarettes and boxes of candy bars.

More than fifty lifeboats and life rafts were set adrift between the dispersal point and the coast of Novaya Zemlya. Men aboard them refused to leave when hailed from the decks of Allied ships. The ships were going to be sunk anyhow, they said. It would do no good to go aboard.

But in every ship there were men who fought right to the end, and five were so well handled they escaped the Germans. *Troubador*, a ship of Panamanian registry with a United States Navy gun crew aboard, was one that saved herself. She was commanded by Captain George J. Salvesen, and her gunnery officer was Ensign H. E. Carraway. The freighter carried tanks on deck that were consigned to the Red Army for service on the Leningrad front. They would never reach Leningrad, though, the ensign knew, unless they were used here first.

The ensign talked with Captain Salvesen on the bridge of *Troubador*. The captain, an old-timer with years of peacetime service in these waters, gave his immediate consent. Ensign Carraway passed the word, and Armed Guard gunners opened up two of the tanks and went inside. While they tried the firing mechanisms and sights of the 37-millimeter guns, cargo was broached and suitable ammunition taken from it.

When the next Heinkel torpedo bomber came carelessly close in attack, it was met by double blasts of tank-gun fire. Severe damage was done to the plane, and *Troubador* took care of herself for the rest of the run into Novaya Zemlya.

Five ships from the convoy, *Troubador* among them, entered the Matochkin Strait and went as far as possible into the ice field. They would be protected from the Germans by both the ice, which prevented the U-boats from getting at them, and the high mountain ridges of Novaya Zemlya. This was on the afternoon of July 6, and the next day they were joined there by four other vessels, all survivors of the German attacks.

Captain Salvesen had already started to paint *Troubador*'s decks and hull white and to use sheets as further camouflage. He urged the other shipmasters to take the same action. They agreed, and the huddled line of ships was camouflaged along the seaward side. A German patrol plane missed them, pulled away over the mountains and did not return.

The ships were able to leave a few days later, and on July 25 the group reached Archangel. There were in that port and at various places in the Kola Inlet near Murmansk about 1,300 survivors whose ships had been sunk. The number included 581 Americans. A total of twenty-two out of thirty-three ships had gone to the bottom, taking along 123,000 tons of cargo. The convoy had started out with 188,000 tons.

Clerks at the War Shipping Administration were busy after the detailed PQ-17 reports reached Washington. They mailed out a printed communication which bore at the end the name "E. S. Land, Administrator." The spaces were filled in by the clerks so that the correct relationship terms and names were used. It read:

"We know that words of condolence can be of little comfort to you in your grief for the death of your brave . . . , . . . , but we want you to feel we share in your sorrow. As truly as any member of our Armed Forces who is killed in battle your . . . gave his life for our country and the cause for which it fights—the hope of freedom on this earth for all mankind. . . . It takes iron fortitude and indifference to danger to be a good merchant seaman in this war. Their duty is to face— on every voyage—the constant threat of death, and go on with their work accepting this threat as the commonplace risk of a day's job. . . ."

Hitler published his own communication about PQ-17 and the work of Operation Knight's Gambit. This was made part of a manual issued to the German fleet. The title was *Convoy Slaughter in the Arctic Sea.*

THE severity of the losses suffered by the PQ-17 convoy stopped until September any Allied effort to send supplies over the North Cape route to Murmansk and Archangel. Then, in the next convoy, PQ-18, the merchant ships were much more heavily armed. They were given twenty-millimeter Oerlikon quick-firing pieces, and three-inch and five-inch cannon. Escort was also increased and stayed with the convoy all the way.

German attacks were savage and numerous, but were beaten off after considerable ship damage. PQ-18 got through with the greater part of its ships intact, and the convoys that followed it met less resistance. Ships were able to run by themselves, unescorted, during the season of arctic darkness, and most of them made the voyage unharmed. Hitler was still aware of the importance of the route, but his attention had been diverted far to the south. The invasion of North Africa had begun and threatened to restore to the Allies the immense areas of Mediterranean territory Hitler and the Italians had seized in the early days of the war.

Operation Torch was the code name for the North African invasion. It had been planned for months, after consultations between Roosevelt and Churchill and with the grudging assent of Stalin, who looked upon it as a poor substitute for an invasion of western Europe. The armada gathered for the assault was the greatest in modern maritime history. There were 102 naval and merchant ships that made rendezvous on October 20, 1942, in the middle of the Atlantic, then proceeded on a zigzag, evasive course until they reached a point off the coast of North Africa.

German intelligence had been completely fooled, and without enemy knowledge the convoy formed into nine columns and five rows, occupying twenty by thirty miles of sea space. The vessels steamed a thousand yards apart, the big new battleship *Massachusetts* in the van, and back astern the famous cruiser *Augusta*. Guarding the flanks were bulky, broad *Texas* and *New York*, veteran battleships. The cruiser *Brooklyn* kept contact between the main body of the convoy and the Air Group, stationed twelve miles astern. This element consisted of the aircraft carrier *Ranger*, four escort carriers, the cruiser *Cleveland*, and nine destroyers.

The flagship was *Augusta*, with Rear Admiral Henry Kent Hewitt, USN, in command. A special screen of forty destroyers protected her and the transports, the cargo vessels, and the tankers in the center of the convoy. Merchant seamen, even old-timers who had seen service in World War I, were awed. Here was a tremendously powerful force, bound on a mission of supreme importance.

Secrecy had been strictly maintained and the convoy objectives only revealed at sea. The masters of the main body of thirty-five ships, the big, gray-painted transports and cargo vessels and tankers realized then how much of a gamble had been taken at Allied headquarters.

The convoy steamed at fourteen knots holding zigzag, evasive courses, and well covered by aircraft, the escort screen fully protective. There were three objectives. The first was Safi, a small port on the African coast below Casablanca; then Fedala, twelve miles away from the large military and naval bases at Casablanca; and then Port Lyautey, to the east of Casablanca, where the French operated the only year-round airstrip in North Africa.

The enemy would be the French troops who had accepted German control through orders issued from Occupied France. They were an unknown quantity; how hard they might fight. and how long, could only be guessed until the actual landings were made. But Casablanca was a wealthy city with a population of 250,000, modern port facilities and large military installations. It was highly valuable as a key to the invasion of the Mediterranean. If the French fought with all their available strength to hold it, and if weather conditions were not right for the main landing at Fedala, the operation could readily fail.

There were 35,000 troops in the American transports. The ships that carried them were former passenger liners, known in peacetime for their luxurious accommodations. Now the soldiers were jammed into narrow compartments, most of which were below the water line. They occupied bunks that were stacked five deep, and one man's boots were in the next man's face. Dice and poker games went on without a break; sometimes as much as ten thousand dollars was bet on a single roll of the dice.

During the first few days at sea, fair weather held, but on November 4 it blew hard from the northwest. The troop compartments became sour-smelling prisons for the GI's, and even up on the ships' bridges in the open air young officers were violently seasick. But the change in the weather created another, much more serious problem. It could delay or completely halt the operation. Landing craft would not be able to go ashore onto the exposed Moroccan beaches in rough, high seas.

The convoy kept course and speed and feinted toward Gibraltar as if to enter the Mediterranean. Then, taking the chance that the weather would abate, it headed straight for the Moroccan objectives. Two other Allied convoys that carried 100,000 men of a British-American force were on the way from United Kingdom ports. Their orders were to penetrate the Mediterranean and make landings at Oran and Algiers. Time was now too short for a revision of the attack plans.

Watch officers in the long rows of Morocco-bound ships were extremely tense that last night at sea. The landings were scheduled to begin right after midnight on November 8 and to continue into daylight. Down on deck, the lashings on the Higgins landing boats were being loosened, and gunners stood motionless in the darkness. The bridges were dark, too, and the light necessary in the wheelhouses subdued and kept to an absolute minimum.

When an officer came in from a bridge wing he put out his hands to grope his way. Small strips of luminous tape had been stuck on the bridge telegraph, and the compass binnacle, the gyroscopic repeater compass, the whistle handle. The clock on the forward bulkhead was softly illuminated, and the revolution counter. There was a thin wedge of light from the compass that the wheelsman used for his steering, and the man's face dimly showed.

But for the mate just in from the total darkness of the bridge where his eyes had become almost permanently adjusted to long distances, they were hardly enough. His eyes were not yet refocused and as he bumped into various objects and people, he kept saying, "Sorry! I'm sorry."

It was better back out on the bridge with the night binoculars trained on the ships ahead and, more and more often, on the black mass of the Moroccan shore to starboard. That over there, the pale loom against the sky, was Casablanca, and this side of it was El Hank lighthouse. El Hank was completely dark, but according to the intelligence reports, it was flanked by 75-millimeter batteries, and French gunners were surely on duty beside their weapons.

The convoy kept on unchallenged, and the main force took position soon after midnight off Fedala and got ready for assault. Invasion day, November 8, broke fair, but with haze over the moderate ground swell. Transports were hoisting out their landing boats, sending troops down the cargo nets over the sides. The Coast Guard coxswains and crews in the landing craft shoved rapidly for the shore, and now guns began to speak.

UNQUIET PACIFIC. An Army assault transport, the USS *Cambria*, built originally as a Maritime Commission C-3 cargo vessel, waits her turn to discharge her troops off an island beachhead. Her masts are festooned with radar

gear and yardarms for several sets of signal halyards. Her main deck swarms with soldiers carrying packs, rifles, and combat orders. Boat ropes hang over her sides, ready for the landing craft that will take the men ashore.

The French were fighting. They did not accept the Americans as their allies. Destroyers and cruisers were engaged with French warships off Casablanca. The big and powerful French battle cruiser *Jean Bart* fired long range salvos from her berth in Casablanca harbor and was answered by *Massachusetts*, *Texas*, and *New York*. Planes from *Ranger* and the other carriers whipped over the city, bombed and strafed the busy 75-millimeter batteries at El Hank, swept on eastward along the coast and gave a hand at Fedala and at Port Lyautey.

There was severe infantry fighting inshore from the Fedala beaches, but it did not last long. The neat little town and the French military installations were secured by noon. Reports from the other attack forces were good. The landing at Safi had gone well, and that port was secured. There had been trouble at Port Lyautey, with ships scuttled by the French in the narrow windings of the Oued Sebou River and galling fire from ashore. Troops had landed, though, and taken their objectives.

Men began to relax in the fleet of fifteen ships off Fedala. Troops and supplies were being sent to the beaches in a steady fashion. French naval vessels still made occasional sorties from Casablanca and exchanged bursts with the American destroyers and cruisers, but *Jean Bart* had been silenced by a thousand-pound bomb delivered onto her foredeck by a plane off *Ranger*.

This was pretty much all right, the Operation Torch crews told themselves. The combined British-American forces inside Gibraltar at Oran and Algiers were having a really hard time. They had met fierce opposition, but here the French were just about ready to capitulate.

Then a U-boat moved past the destroyer screen and through the mine field on the night of November 11 and attacked in Fedala Roads the transport *Joseph Hewes*. She went down taking nearly all of her cargo with her. While general-alarm bells sounded and gunners ran to battle stations aboard the American ships, the U-boat maneuvered for further attack. The Navy tanker *Winooski* was hit, and a destroyer, but they were able to stay afloat.

The U-boat got away, and with darkness the next day men waited nervously for the enemy craft to return. It came, sliding in and around the shoreward end of the mine field. The submarine was later identified as *U-130*, and her crew were highly trained.

U-130 delivered four torpedoes from her bow tubes, swung and sent another from her stern tube. All those found targets. They struck, set afire, and sank the transports *Edward Rutledge*, *Tasker H. Bliss*, and *Hugh L. Scott*. Hundreds of people were left floundering in the water to be saved by landing craft, launches, and lifeboats from the rest of the fleet. But *U-130* escaped, and 111 American lives were lost.

Sadness came to the merchant seamen who had witnessed the swift, skillful German slaughter. It replaced their sense of elation over the victory just won. When they were free from their work of caring for the survivors, they recalled that the ships sunk here had been some of the most famous prewar American passenger liners. They remembered the long list of ships taken by the enemy in the Atlantic, the Caribbean, the Pacific, and along the North Russia route. They wondered how many more would be lost in these waters, and then in the Mediterranean, and in the final, inevitable assault upon the German-held beaches in western Europe. The future stretched bleak, dark, shadowed by death.

Transports and cargo ships moved from the Fedala anchorage right after the *U-130* attack. Dock space was found in Casablanca harbor by the suddenly obliging French authorities. But the American ships entered at Casablanca an oil-slopped litter in which bodies of men killed in action bumped with the tide against the breakwaters. More than twenty ships had been scuttled inside the mole by the French Navy, and on the bottom with them were scuttled French submarines and a huge drydock that had been punctured by many rounds of large-caliber U.S. Navy gunfire.

The city looked very good after the tension at sea. The merchant seamen, along with the Army and Navy men from Operation Torch, explored it until all available liquor had been drunk and certain sections were declared off limits. Casablanca, with its handsome, wide boulevards, rows of palm trees, stately public buildings, and fine hotels, soon assumed a madhouse atmosphere.

Snipers fired from the roofs of apartment houses at night, concentrating on the brilliantly lighted dock area where cargo-ship crews discharged ammunition. The drunken and unwary who defied the blackout regulations and wandered around in the city were often discovered with their throats cut and were invariably robbed. Gangs of men and women and scrawny, sharp-eyed children gathered at the barbed-wire barriers of the port area and bargained in broken English. Fantastic deals were arranged for stolen ships' sheets and pillowcases, butter, sugar, cigarettes and candy.

Cargo had been piled on the docks helter-skelter in the first days of the occupation. It was either stolen by people whom the merchant seamen loosely called "Ay-rabs," or it rotted, rusted, and disintegrated where it lay. There was one notorious heap on the Quai des Phosphates that contained three sections of steel matting, a case of Wiener schnitzel, two ten-gallon field containers of aviation gasoline, a case of pistol ammunition, a field container of lubricating oil, a case of strawberry jam, and several rounds of 105-millimeter incendiary ammunition.

This enormous waste was to be repeated in many ports around the world during the course of the war. Men who had risked their lives to haul the cargo were to become accustomed to the sight. But here it was new and startling and aroused grave doubt. They asked themselves if the "people topside" in Washington really knew how to run a war.

Back in New York and the other East Coast loading ports, the crews that returned from North Africa heard stories of ships which had distinguished themselves in action. The Allied theater of operations was steadily expanding in the Mediterranean. But Rommel's *Afrika Korps* veterans fought hard, and made up for the lapses of the Italian forces who thought more of surrender than of an Axis victory. The *Luftwaffe* was very active, too, and caused great damage to ships in convoy and at anchor or docked in the crowded ports.

The Liberty ship *Virginia Dare*, whose gunners had shot down eight German planes during the September, 1942, convoy passage to North Russia, was less fortunate on her next voyage. While in the Mediterranean she was torpedoed and almost sunk. Her crew stuck with her; she was beached, and her valuable cargo saved.

Another Liberty ship, *Samuel Parker*, was assigned to ferry service between Egyptian and Tunisian ports during a rough phase of the desert campaign. She carried troops and ammunition, and before the Germans were through with her she received 130 holes in her hull and superstructure.

Her wooden bulkheads were blown out, and her steel doors sprung by concussion. During a fierce *Luftwaffe* attack upon Tripoli harbor, British soldiers lined her rails along the main deck and with their rifle fire helped to defend her. Ships were set afire all around her; and she was set afire.

The chief mate, Storkersen, and an able-bodied sailor, Anderson, went down into the forehold and doused the fire that had started in the ammunition stowed there. Then they went aft, strapping on foamite extinguishers. Another fire threatened the cargo in the afterhold—cased gasoline. They put it out, too, and took up other duties.

Two men of the *Samuel Parker* crew had been killed and several wounded. But a fireman-watertender named Vrem took along with him in the ship's motor-powered lifeboat four volunteers. A British ship alongside the Liberty had been struck and was on fire. Vrem and his shipmates were able to save six men from the British crew.

For this and other action in the area, *Samuel Parker* was given the first Gallant Ship award* by the War Shipping Administration. Her master, Captain Elmer J. Stoll, was awarded the Merchant Marine Distinguished Service Medal, and Storkersen and Anderson, the chief officer and

---

* There is at the end of this book a full list of World War II Gallant Ship awards.

the able-bodied sailor who had fought the fire, were given the same decoration. Vrem, for some reason, was overlooked.

The North Russia run and the dangers met there brought distinction to *William Moultrie* and her entire ship's company. She was a Liberty caught in the awful ordeal of the September, 1942, convoy. Her master was Captain Richard E. Hocken, and for the way he handled her he was given the Merchant Marine Distinguished Service Medal.

William Moultrie was attacked thirteen times by low-flying German torpedo planes and higher-level bombers. She was credited with a score of eight planes shot down, smashed into the sea, and direct hits on twelve more. During the first attack, she shot out of the air three torpedo planes and assisted in the destruction of six others. She dumped four more the next day and damaged five.

There was a later attack in which four German torpedoes were sighted close to the ship and headed for the stern. Warning was given to Captain Hocken on the bridge. The ship's course was instantly changed and the after gun brought to bear on the nearest torpedo. It was exploded by a shell from the three-inch, fifty-caliber cannon, and Captain Hocken maneuvered clear of the others that followed.

Ensign Mahoney, commander of the Armed Guard detachment, was decorated with the Silver Star by the United States Navy for his part in this action. The twenty-four men of his detachment were awarded the Navy Unit Citation, and the vessel was given the Gallant Ship award by the War Shipping Administration.

But heroism in action and recognition of it could not

compensate for the great lack of merchant marine manpower. Too many veteran masters, mates, engineers, and seamen of all ratings had been killed during the first year of the war. The figure for the dead and missing was put at 3,200 by Elmer Davis, Director of the Office of War Information, in an announcement made early in 1943. He stated also that the merchant marine had suffered a casualty toll of almost four percent in comparison with less than one percent for the armed forces.

The government increased its already intensive campaign to recruit and train seamen. The ships were waiting, and the cargoes, and every day the sea routes to the war fronts grew longer.

chapter 9

OLD-TIME sailors had already pointed out to War Shipping Administration officials that dry land was no place to train a man for the sea. But the government, because of war conditions along both coasts and in the Gulf of Mexico, had little choice. The best it could do was establish the training bases alongside salt-water bays and tidal rivers.

No further delay was possible. A quarter of a million additional seamen had to be sent aboard. No doubt many of them would be still green, and would arouse both the rage and despair of their veteran shipmates. But what they had failed to learn ashore they would pick up at sea. It would still take four times as long to train a seaman as it did to build a ship.

NOT LONG NOW. A Liberty ship has been struck by a dive bomber. She is badly afire, and her ammunition is threatened. The small craft astern are picking up sur-

vivors. The Navy gunners can only stand and watch and brace themselves for the explosion.

The United States Maritime Service, the uniformed training branch of the merchant marine, expanded from its six prewar installations to more than two hundred across the nation. A muster of 5,200 officer cadets were sent to government schools at Kings Point, New York; Pass Christian, Mississippi; and San Mateo, California. Great care was taken with their training. These young men, between the ages of eighteen and twenty-three years, were to replace the veteran officers who had been lost at sea. They were in a very strict sense invaluable.

During their first two months of basic training they remained ashore. Then for periods of from six to eight months they went to sea and learned fast and hard. The final part of their instruction was in advanced courses of six to eight months at the United States Merchant Marine Academy at Kings Point. With graduation, they were qualified to sit for licenses as third mates or third assistant engineers. They were also eligible upon receiving their licenses to serve as ensigns in the United States Navy.

Captain Giles C. Stedman, tall and handsome, a veteran peacetime shipmaster with a splendid record, was the second officer to become superintendent of the Merchant Marine Academy at Kings Point. He succeeded another highly respected veteran, Captain James H. Tomb, who had been forced to retire because of ill health. Between them, they instilled in the cadets a sense of service tradition that was never to be lost at sea. Kings Point cadets distinguished themselves often during the course of the war, and a number gave their lives.

Five state maritime academies, all under federal supervision, helped meet the officer shortage. They enrolled an aggregate of 1,000 cadets in 1942, and their superintendents reported to Washington that they planned to graduate approximately 1,500 in 1943 and a similar number in 1944. These were schools established before the war, with seasoned staffs and a great deal of practical training equipment. They were situated at San Francisco, California; Castine, Maine; Hyannis, Massachusetts; Philadelphia, Pennsylvania; and right across from Kings Point, the New York State Maritime Academy at Fort Schuyler, in the Bronx, New York.

But the demand was not at all satisfied by the number of graduates from the various academies. Thousands of qualified men had to be put on the bridges and into the engine rooms of seagoing ships in much less time than that taken by academy training. The Maritime Service looked to the veteran seamen who could be recruited straight from the ships and sent back as officers after a short, intensive course of instruction.

The Coast Guard had handled during the first phase of the war the instruction of merchant seamen who sought to become licensed officers. Now, at the end of 1942, the Maritime Service assumed the responsibility. Two Maritime Service schools were set up, one at Fort Trumbull, New London, Connecticut, and the other at Alameda, California, across the bay from San Francisco. Requirements for entrance were only that a man have fourteen months of sea service behind him; he could be of any age, and any scholastic background.

Men in the ships were diffident at first and called the schools, with some scorn, "mate factories." They said that they were unwilling to cram so much into their skulls in a four-month period of instruction, then come back aboard, "move midships and wear a high-pressure hat." Then, though, they started to enroll with the pressure of their own ships' officers, their families, and their unions upon them.

Most of the lot, of course, had never finished high school. Concentrated learning was new to them, and very difficult. They had been bombed, strafed, torpedoed, adrift in boats and rafts, and under unremitting strain since the beginning of the war. Discipline for them belonged at sea and definitely not ashore. While they were called "mister" by their instructors, rated as chief petty officers, and paid $126 a month, they were uneasy. They did not like going around to classrooms with piles of books under their arms, and they wanted to go back to sea.

More than a third of these men dropped out of the officer-candidate schools before their courses were finished. For this, in some official circles in Washington, the merchant marine was criticized. But the men who left Fort Trumbull and Alameda did not leave the sea. They returned to the ships as bosuns, quartermasters, able-bodied seamen, pumpmen, oilers, and fireman-watertenders. Some, until the end of the war, put on their Maritime Service uniforms when going ashore; they were proud to wear them. It showed, to the wearers at least, that they had done their best.

A strange current of dislike of the merchant marine persisted and increased, though, as the war progressed. The source of it in part came from certain high-ranking Navy officers who had believed right along that the merchant marine should not be an independent service. The maritime unions were criticized, their actions called unpatriotic, and a great deal was said about undue amounts of overtime pay, the laxity of various crews while at sea, drunkenness, insubordination, and Communism. The merchant marine should belong to the Navy, the high-ranking officers said; then all of that would stop.

Their contention was picked up by several national newspapers and periodicals which attacked the merchant marine, as far as could be discovered, because of antiunion sentiment. *Time Magazine* in its December 21, 1942, issue let go with a particularly virulent blast which could only have had a very bad effect upon the national war effort. *Time* saw fit to print:

10,000 men between the ages of 17 and 35 who customarily greet each other as "Slacker," "Draft-dodger" and "Profiteer," stood for one and a half hours in the icy offshore wind at the United States Maritime Training Station at Sheepshead Bay, N.Y., last week and heard themselves lauded by President Roosevelt (by letter) and a No. 2 company of lauders as potentially gallant merchant seamen. To the undisguised relief of the station's 1,800 instructors, they uttered no boo, and only a few rude mutterings.

Thus was inaugurated the country's largest merchant marine training school: $14,000,000 ﹐ worth of plant and equipment spread over 310 acres of what once was a honky-tonk amusement park, Manhattan Beach. The training school is geared to turn out 40,000 basically-trained sailors a year.

Rough and rambunctious, uniformed as sailors but fully aware that their civilian status permits nose-thumbing at MP's, the 13-week volunteer trainees sneer at their $50-a-month pay, wait for the day they sign on for double pay of $200 a month, or $250 for those qualifying for higher ratings. . . .

The article drew a sharp reply from Captain Macauley of the War Shipping Administration. He sent a telegram to *Time* which vigorously defended the trainees enrolled at Sheepshead Bay. The last paragraph of Captain Macauley's message read: "Some of these men will give their lives to protect those of us who stay at home—including the author of your attack."

The Sheepshead Bay base continued to turn out thousands of young men who were routed through the maritime unions to ships and almost immediate sea duty. There were other such schools for unlicensed personnel at Hoffman Island in the lower bay of the Port of New York; and at St. Petersburg, Florida; Avalon, California; Huntington, New York; and Gallup's Island, in Boston harbor. Wearing a dismal imitation of a United States Navy enlisted man's uniform, the trainees became a familiar sight in the major American ports.

A number of them were loudmouthed and had picked up much too quickly extensive seagoing vocabularies and the manners of veteran sailors. Others had no intention at all of going to sea; they were unquestionably draft dodgers and malingerers. Some, carried away by a desire to appear heroic, bought decorations and service ribbons in hock shops and bedizened themselves with row on row. This charade was stopped when the Maritime Service created its own Shore Patrol to round up and arrest if necessary the "performers" who had begun to give the merchant marine a bad name. But one young trainee had already hung on his chest and worn in public a Boer War medal. He had paid, he told the Shore Patrol, a dollar for it.

The Maritime Service training program although badly impeded at first by wasteful methods and an overabundance of instructors, functioned well in the latter part of the war. Trainees who had gone to sea wearing their uniforms and shocked veteran mates by a hand salute when given an order on deck returned home changed men. They now had an understanding of war, and they no longer needed the semimilitary trappings. A civilian suit was good enough ashore, that and having taken a ship to sea.

chapter **10**

D URING the winter of 1942-43, men who were back in their home ports used a new phrase. It was "inside the Straits," and by that was meant the Mediterranean past the Straits of Gibraltar. The United States was finding crews for her merchant ships. There were to be five hundred vessels hauling troops and cargo into the narrow, historic sea before the end of hostilities, and from December, 1942, until July, 1943, nearly all unloading was done under enemy attack.

The toll of ships lost to the enemy continued to be heavy. *Luftwaffe* squadrons concentrated their attacks upon the shipping in the various badly congested port areas. Fast-flying Italian planes also participated in some raids, and the pride of the Mussolini navy was the record made by its "frogmen." The Italian frogmen, all volunteers and extremely daring, were skillful underwater demolition experts who delighted in attaching electrically operated mines to the sides of Allied ships. They were aided in their attempts by swift motor launches, a version of the American PT boat, that recklessly assaulted harbor defenses with torpedoes and small-caliber cannon fire while bombs were being swum into position by the underwater crews.

Doenitz kept his men hard at work along the Atlantic routes, off Gibraltar, and in the Mediterranean, anywhere an Allied ship could be found. There was no doubt among American seamen that the U-boats received fuel, supplies, and ammunition in the Spanish ports, along with a warm welcome. Convoys that ran off the Spanish mainland or the coast of Spanish Morocco were attacked time and again by U-boats which when pursued by the escort used a simple tactic to escape. The U-boat commanders took their vessels into Spanish territorial waters, and the Allied warships were forced to withdraw, afraid of an accusation of having violated international law.

One of Doenitz's victims while headed for the Mediterranean was the sturdy American ship *City of Flint*. She had been seized and then released by the Germans in the early days of the war before the United States was a participant. But she was already famous for her work in 1939, when she had answered the distress call of the steamer *Athenia*. She was known as a lucky ship after that, until a U-boat finished her.

She was sunk by torpedo attack on January 25, 1943, and went down flaming. Seventeen men were lost. The rest, in-

INSIDE THE ATOLL. A Coast Guard gunner stands alert on watch aboard an American Merchant Marine supply ship after Kwajelein has been taken in assault from the Japanese. This is part of General MacArthur's plan to

cluding military personnel, got away in the lifeboats. A survivor reported that the ship's radio operator sent out distress signals after *City of Flint* was gone. He had swum from the sinking ship to a lifeboat and lugged along a portable radio set.

Torpedo and bomb damage became common for ships in the Mediterranean service. Seamen just a few weeks out of the Stateside training schools were veterans after a single voyage. They had learned how to handle cargo gear during direct enemy attack and keep on at their work in the engine rooms and firerooms. while the bulkheads resounded with the slam of bombs, pumps jumped and missed a

recover the islands, and soon the ships will head westward from the Marshalls toward the Caroline group, then to the Marianas and the Philippines.

stroke, and lights flickered as the generators pulsated with shock.

The grim, slow, often stupid business of war formed a pattern in the Mediterranean. There were the fire-scorched and beached ships in the outer roadsteads, then, inside the mine-gates, the closely packed ships that discharged cargo onto the battered docks or lay empty and already rusted, waiting for convoy to be made up for home. The port towns were nearly all white-walled and red-roofed, the natives in most cases unfriendly and incomprehensible.

Air attacks came usually at night, and it did not matter much whether the port was Oran, or Bône, or Palermo, or a dozen others in between them. Tracers tore the sky. Parachute flares guttered above the ships, and the guns and the bombs clashed in a shuddering roar. Incendiary pellets, small, cherry red, rolled along the decks, were kicked overside or doused with sand. Ships were struck, caught fire, exploded, and men in a frenzy of haste performed rescue work which they never fully remembered afterward.

The United States Navy salvage crews under the direction of Commodore William A. Sullivan performed incredible work in the ports, cleared them of enemy-laid mines, undetonated bombs and shells and sunken ships. They worked gallantly, too, saving ships that had been set afire, hauled many of these vessels out of the crowded port areas where an explosion would have frightful, chain-action effects. A number of Commodore Sullivan's fire-fighter crew members had served before the war in the New York City Fire Department. But their skill sometimes led them to take extreme risks. Several lost their lives when burning ships exploded under them before they could get away to the rescue tugs.

The Allied landings had begun to spread forth across the Mediterranean, from Africa to Sicily, and then the Italian mainland. Merchant marine crews discharged their ships in Palermo, and on the next voyage lay off the bitterly held Salerno beachhead while the German 88's fired salvo after salvo from the olive groves on the hills, and Allied destroyers and cruisers, as close to the beach as they could get, returned the barrage. Then it was Naples, the harbor wrecked and mined by the Germans before their retreat, *Luftwaffe* planes coming in low from the cloud banks along the red lava slopes of Vesuvius.

With Palermo and the rest of Sicily secured, the Suez Canal could again be freely used by Allied shipping. American merchant ships were taken from the "Straits shuttle" to the Mediterranean. They were dispatched in late 1943 and throughout the rest of the war to ports of call all over the world. They carried cargoes to India and to the Persian Gulf for transshipment overland to the Soviet Union. Liberty ships still wearing their first coats of paint sailed alone around the Cape of Good Hope, bound for Madagascar and the Red Sea, or Australia and New Zealand.

Others were routed through the Panama Canal to evade the U-boats that still patrolled the South Atlantic. They ran down the west coast of South America and rounded Cape Horn. It was a perilous passage, but not in the way it had been for the old sailing ships heavily hurt by storms. Here in the desolate, lonely reaches of the Pacific off the lower part of the South American mainland, German surface raiders waited.

The German Navy had started surface-raider operations in January, 1940, with seven heavily armed vessels and their supporting tankers and supply ships. The raiders were all former passenger liners with plenty of space for their armament of six 5.9-inch cannon and either four or six torpedo tubes. Small scout planes and hundreds of mines that were systematically strewn at the entrances to enemy harbors were carried aboard.

The German ships were cleverly camouflaged, could be made to resemble half a dozen types by raising or lowering canvas bulkheads and false stacks, masts, and derricks. Their average speed was nineteen knots, and below decks were water and fuel tanks that gave them a cruising range

of almost seventy thousand miles. Some of the raider crews
mustered as many as 350 men, hard-bitten veterans carefully chosen for this duty.

Rendezvous points for the raiders, their supply vessels,
and U-boats sent out by Doenitz were established in both
the South Atlantic and the Indian Ocean. One was halfway between Capetown and the northern Argentine coast.
The other was in the middle of the Indian Ocean, within
easy striking distance of the main British-American ship
routes.

With their scout planes, their ability to change appearance quickly, and their relatively high rate of speed, the
raiders escaped Allied pursuit for some time. They sank the
unescorted ships, mostly freighters or tankers, without
mercy and without excess gunfire.

There were only a few survivors from the sunken ships. A
great part of the Allied crews were killed early in the Nazi
attacks. The men who went into boats or aboard rafts
drifted until, slowly, they died—food, water, and hope
gone.

The full count of the Nazi raider destruction in the war
was eighty-six American ships. Across the area between the
Cape of Good Hope, Cape Horn, and the South Cape of
New Zealand, in what the sailors called "the low latitudes," a million and a half tons of Allied shipping were
sunk. The Germans were responsible for almost all of this
loss, although they fought fifteen thousand miles away from
home when on duty in the Pacific. They were much more
effective at any phase of the operation than their Japanese
allies.

It was an alert German raider crew on duty in the South

Atlantic that caught on June 6, 1942, the tanker *Stanvac Calcutta*. They engaged her in an unequal fight which could only end with the tanker's destruction. But *Stanvac Calcutta*, of Panamanian registry, carried a United States Navy gun crew.

The action was fought fifty miles off the Brazilian coast, and the tanker ran alone. The Nazi vessel emerged out of thick rain squalls, closed, cleared her 5.9-inch guns, and without a challenge began to fire. *Stanvac Calcutta* mounted a four-inch cannon aft and a three-inch gun forward. She was swung to bring the four-incher to bear on the enemy.

Headway was kept on both vessels as they fought. The young gunners aboard *Stanvac Calcutta* laid their four-incher well. They knocked out one of the Germans' big pieces. But the next round from the raider caused severe damage. The sight bar and the pointer's scope on the four-inch piece were shattered. It was difficult to serve the weapon without them. The gunners kept on firing until the ship, holed all along her hull, started to sink under them, and the ammunition locker was hit.

Stanvac Calcutta lost fourteen dead, and fourteen of her people were seriously wounded. When she was abandoned, the men in the boats were threatened by small-arms fire from the raider. They were taken prisoner and finished the war in Milag Nord, the German prison camp for merchant seamen outside Bremerhaven.

The Liberty ship *Stephen Hopkins* was found by a pair of German raiders in similar circumstances in the same region and ruthlessly sunk. This was in September, 1942, and it was then that Cadet Edwin O'Hara distinguished himself defending his ship and lost his life.

The raiders on Pacific Ocean duty moved busily along the Allied ship routes that led westward from the Panama Canal. Their choice targets were the tankers that headed unescorted and deep-laden in Venezuelan oil for Honolulu and ports thousands of miles beyond it to satisfy the needs of the United States Navy, Army, and Air Force. Ships bound for Guadalcanal and the other distant islands were met by the raiders and easily, quickly destroyed. Radio warnings from the attacked vessels were rarely completed; enemy gunfire stopped them, and the raiders' positions went unreported.

But then British and American naval units began a wide search. The raiders were hunted systematically, and trapped, sunk, rendered useless, left beached or badly wrecked. They were the last of their kind. Germany lacked the vessels and the crews to replace them. It was the U-boats working with the *Luftwaffe* which harassed American shipping to the end of the war.

But in the Aleutian campaign, fought in the chill northern Pacific waters off Alaska, where Liberties participated with former passenger liners, the Japanese were the enemy. The landings at Attu and Kiska were made between March 24 and August 15, 1943, when Japanese resistance collapsed. Men in the American merchant crews were very glad to leave the area. The Liberty ships were of welded construction and a number of them, due to faulty shipyard work and the rapid changes between air and sea temperatures, split in half. This usually happened at the Number Three hold bulkhead and almost invariably without warning.

"There we was," a survivor from a Liberty ship sinking reported later in San Francisco. "More than fifty of us, some guys still in their shirt tails, swimming around like seals. I'll take Esperitu Santo first, or old Guadal', instead of that."

General MacArthur was on his way back toward the Philippines, and in greatly increasing numbers ships were sent to supply the southwestern Pacific island bases held by American troops. Liberty ships that had loaded in New York or Baltimore or Philadelphia and had traversed the Panama Canal and T-2 tankers with bunker fuel or aviation gasoline taken aboard in the Persian Gulf lay for weeks in the island roadsteads waiting to discharge.

Men became familiar with every characteristic of the Japanese planes, the fast, low-diving Zeroes and the more clumsy, slower bombers called Bettys. Life aboard ship was spent as much as possible out on deck. The forecastles stunk, and were stifling, and there was nothing to be done about it; blackout regulations kept the portholes tightly sealed and long, thick curtains at every exit onto deck.

Bunks were lifted from their frames in the fo'c'sles and carried out on deck after permission had been granted by the master and the gunnery officer. Some men stretched their mattresses out across the cargo hatches, although they understood that if the ship were attacked pressure from a bomb blast would send them hurtling high along with the hatch boards. There were also the sleepless men, found in every crew. They prowled the main deck, listening to the jungle sounds from ashore, the birds that barked like dogs, the monkeys that screamed, and the burst of rifle fire from overnervous sentries.

During the day, heat went over 100 degrees Fahrenheit. A mist of fumes, reeking and extremely dangerous, hung over the spar decks of tankers while they lay waiting to discharge. Their deck plates were so hot that men in thick-soled GI boots walked quickly to the next bit of shade. Booby birds circled cautiously away, returned to the jungle where steam from the rotted vegetation rose above the huge, dark trees in an impenetrable white wall.

Some ships lay at the southwest Pacific anchorages for months before they were unloaded. Men turned yellow-skinned from repeated doses of atabrine against malaria. Their hair fell out and their teeth loosened; they suffered from fungus growth on their bodies, from a diet which had become absolutely monotonous no matter what the cooks tried to do with it, and from homesickness.

The homesickness was worst of all. Long hours were spent in writing letters which men tore up and then re-wrote. Mail call was nerve-wracking, often tragic. Men who had failed to receive letters broke down and wept, and sometimes attempted suicide.

Shore leave in most of the Pacific outposts was impossible. Fighting was often close to the beaches, and Japanese snipers hid in tall trees that offered them shots at bathers and ballplayers. The crews were confined to their ships and endlessly gambled, sorted piles of cowrie shells bought from visiting Navy Seabees, and pawed over fake Japanese battle flags and *samurai* swords, also peddled by Seabees, but furnished, too, by GI's and Marines who toured the harbors in borrowed landing craft. It was only late in the war, in 1944 and 1945, and then on islands that had been long secured, that "jungle show" theaters were built for the entertainment of the troops, and the United Seamen's Service was able to establish a few palm-thatch "clubs" where a merchant seaman could buy himself three cans of beer, sit down, and read Stateside newspapers.

There were hundreds of ships, nearly all of them cargo vessels, held up in various war areas, not only in the far Pacific, but in the Mediterranean and at ports of the United Kingdom, Iceland, and North Russia. Still other ships were kept fantastically busy and were dispatched by the War Shipping Administration to a series of ports around the world. The Liberty ship *Arthur P. Davis* was one of these and made her circumnavigation between August 18, 1943, and April 14, 1944, steaming 32,400 miles. She traversed four of the seven oceans and crossed the equator four times. Along the way, she sank a Japanese submarine, the only United States merchant ship to be so credited.

Arthur P. Davis was built by the California Shipbuilding Company at Terminal Island, in the center of teeming Los Angeles harbor. Her master was Captain John Harris, who had been going to sea for twenty-seven years, and her chief engineer, Robert Remsen, was another veteran officer. The chief mate had not been at sea in eight years, though, and the two junior mates had just graduated from maritime school. Captain Harris looked forward to a long and anxious voyage.

When he cleared the Los Angeles harbor breakwater at 4:00 P.M. on August 18, he was in command of 121 men. His own ship's crew contained eighteen men in the deck department—the chief, second and third mates, the purser, radio operator, bosun, eight able-bodied seamen, and four apprentice seamen; and in the engineering department were thirteen men—Chief Engineer Remsen, the first, second and third assistant engineers, the deck engineer, three oilers, three firemen, and two wipers; there were nine men in the steward's department—the chief steward, the chief cook, the second cook, who also served as baker, three utility men, and three messmen.

The Navy gun crew was commanded by a young ensign named Parker. He had under him a signalman and twenty-five bluejackets. There was also an Army unit of fifty-one men aboard, along with a major and two lieutenants. *Arthur P. Davis* was a crowded ship, and the main part of her cargo was four thousand tons of five-hundred-pound bombs. Captain Harris suspected even before he dropped the pilot and then opened his secret orders that she was bound for an active war zone.

He was right. The orders read for the China-Burma-India theater. His first port of call was Hobart, Tasmania, on a small island off the southeast coast of Australia. The course he laid off for it was 225 degrees. The ship would enter the lonely "low latitudes" where the German surface raiders had made their great score against Allied shipping.

So Captain Harris rigorously trained his crew. There were general-alarm, fire, and boat drills until each man knew his station, could reach it fast, and was thoroughly familiar with his duties as a member of the emergency squads. The ship was armed with ten guns. She had a three-inch fifty-caliber cannon forward and another aft. Eight Oerlikon twenty-millimeter antiaircraft guns were mounted on either side of the ship, six of them on the midships house, and a pair just forward of the after cannon.

This meant a lot of work for the Navy gunners. Men were recruited from the merchant crew and the Army unit to serve as shell passers. Then, with fine weather continuing, gunnery practice was held. The long gray barrels of the cannon swung when the breeches were locked upon the shells, and over the "squawk box" on the bridge the fire order was called by Ensign Parker. The targets were empty fifty-five-gallon drums that were dumped over the side. Gunners, pointers, and trainers learned to work together, to put their fire squarely on the drums and sink them with satisfying regularity.

The Oerlikon gunners, stretching back in their canvas harnesses, the rubber-padded stocks tight against their shoulders, closed the triggers and let go high-sweeping bursts at ten-foot-long meteorological balloons that had been released from the stern of the ship. The fully inflated balloons dipped and swerved and climbed in the wind gusts and were not easy targets. But after five days of gunnery practice, Ensign Parker reported that his men were sufficiently drilled. He would be content now, he told Captain Harris, to conserve the rest of his ammunition, wait to use it on the enemy.

Captain Harris took the broad-bowed Liberty along her course at an average of about three hundred miles a day. During daylight hours he used one of four zigzag patterns issued him at Los Angeles by the Navy before departure. These were changed each day and were designed to keep an enemy submarine from coming within torpedo range of the ship. It was only at night that a straight course was steered and lookouts were kept constantly alert on the main deck.

Arthur P. Davis crossed the equator and reached 52 degrees south latitude, and here Harris set her due west on

HARD STUFF. Landing craft manned by Coast Guards-men come in across Eniwetok Atoll with ammunition for the troops making the final assault in the Marshall group.

Off the beach, at anchor in deep water, are the Merchant Marine supply ships that brought the ammunition from the States.

the last leg for Hobart. She had been nearly a month at sea, and the idea of landfall had begun to look pretty good to all hands. Then, on September 11, she met a storm; it continued and got worse, and by September 13 the barometer was down to 29.22 inches, a reading that meant severe danger for the ship.

They were in the region below the continents, where the winds hurled endlessly and undeflected upon the sea. Huge, long-crested, and cruel waves were formed, which slammed into destruction anything that could not withstand their force. The Liberty ship carried as deck cargo ungainly construction cranes and tanks. They were secured to the deck by a massive network of steel cables, turnbuckles, and pad eyes. But the thrust of the storm shifted them five feet to one side, and up in his cabin as he tried to write a report, Captain Harris was flung to the floor by a particularly rough gust.

He got out on deck to be told by the bosun that one of the lifeboats had been smashed beyond repair. Then the chief mate appeared from the main deck, his seaboots awash, and told about the sidewise movement of the cranes and tanks. There was nothing to be done while the storm lasted, Captain Harris knew. The ship, with 121 men aboard, would have to keep going until she reached port, take her chances with the list caused by the cargo shift and the loss of a lifeboat.

But the weather cleared, and on September 16 the ship came into Hobart. Dock people were incredulous when they looked at the shifted cargo and said the damage was extreme, even for the storms of these latitudes. Captain Harris was glad to grant the crew shore leave for a night;

then fuel and fresh water were taken aboard, the compasses were adjusted, and *Arthur P. Davis* sailed.

The new orders were for Karachi, India, four thousand miles away, and the first leg of the course was almost due west. The ship sailed for two weeks along the underside of Australia, then headed northwest up through the Indian Ocean. This was the "flyin' fish" weather of which the old-time clipper sailors sang in their chanties. Days were an immense white flame above the sheer azure sea; nights were so filled with stars that men could make out their shadows on deck.

War tension still existed, though, and men remained alert. The crow's-nest lookout hailed the bridge smartly on October 12 and reported a pair of Arab dhows ahead. The sailing craft lay side by side about three miles off the Liberty's starboard bow, their sails lowered.

Captain Harris was in his cabin. The second mate, who held the bridge watch, called him by telephone. The captain examined the dhows through his binoculars, ordered the officer to steer well clear of them, and returned to his cabin. But at 2:32 P.M., a few minutes after the first hail, the crow's-nest man bawled down at the bridge:

"Submarine! Lying between those dhows!"

Captain Harris came back to the bridge on the run. Mr. Dorrance, the second mate, had already sounded general alarm and swung the ship, bringing her stern around to present the smallest target to the enemy. Armed Guard men were jumping over the sides of the gun tubs to their weapons. Ensign Parker joined Captain Harris in the wheelhouse, and the master said, "Fire as soon as you're ready."

Ensign Parker shouted into the squawk box, "Number One, open fire!"

That meant the three-inch fifty-caliber cannon forward. She sent a shell whipping aft past the bridge wing while the ship still swung left in answer to the second mate's order. Then she fired another, and another, and in their eagerness to get on target the young gunners almost smacked the corner of the wheelhouse. Captain Parker was forced to tell the ensign, "Secure that gun!"

Parker yelled into the squawk box for the forward gun to cease fire, then called triumphantly to Captain Harris, "We hit him! We got him!"

The submarine lay on the surface between the two dhows. Her conning tower was visible above the calm sea, and the range was less than half a mile. The after three-inch,fifty aboard the Liberty was taking over from the bow cannon. It fired four rounds, and the smooth gray steel of the conning tower and the hull reared in twisted, oil-splashed strips caught by flame.

Ensign Parker gave the cease-fire order to the gunners who handled the after cannon. Mr. Dorrance was in the chart room, plotting the ship's position at the request of the captain. He turned it over to the radio operator. The operator was already at the key of the set in the radio shack and sent out a series of "S" signals along with the ship's call letters, WTZR. That combination in Allied code meant *Arthur P. Davis* had met an enemy submarine.

The radio operator sent his call for fifteen minutes. He failed to get a reply. Karachi, Bombay, and Calcutta were all on the air with routine messages. Ensign Parker asked if the captain would mind if a couple of rounds apiece were tossed into those dhows. The captain said, no, he thought that would be fine.

Two rounds apiece finished the dhows. The ship went back to her course and at 6:37 in the morning, October 14, arrived off Karachi harbor and picked up her pilot. Captain Harris visited Royal Navy headquarters right after he had shaved, taken a shower, and changed into shore clothes.

British officers in their white, short-sleeved shirts, shorts, and knee-length stockings were very pleasant with him. But they were vague about the failure to receive the radio call. "Not to be believed," they told him. "Simply not." The sinking of the submarine, though, that was another matter. It was very certainly to be believed.

A British flying boat and two corvettes had made a close search of the spot. They found a broad oil slick and a mass of debris that contained clothing and boxes with Japanese markings. A boarding party from one of the corvettes had inspected the dhows, and dug out from the bilges Japanese money and rations. There was no doubt that the sailing craft had served as decoys for the submarine.

Captain Harris returned aboard ship and granted the gun crew permission to paint a rising-sun flag and a submarine silhouette on the stack. The Royal Navy had at least confirmed the submarine sinking, even if they kept the excuse machine going hard about the radio call.

Her bomb cargo discharged, and the Army men on their way, *Arthur P. Davis* moved to another dock in Karachi. She took aboard there a load that was consigned to the Russians. It was made up of ammunition, railroad steel, trucks, tanks, medicine, and food. On November 3, when the last of it was stowed the ship moved out and started for the Persian Gulf.

She arrived at Bandar Shahpur on November 8, crossed the bar, and entered the harbor, where thirty ships were waiting to discharge cargo. This was the port that was famous among seamen for the ferocity of its heat. It was hotter than New Guinea, and for hours after darkness men still claimed that they could fry eggs on deck.

But Bandar Shahpur was a vitally important port. Two long steel piers had been built along one side of the harbor, and from it a two-hundred-mile railroad ran north to the Caspian Sea. Cargo loaded aboard ship in the United States and hauled to Bandar Shahpur was unloaded and reloaded on trains that carried it to the Caspian. It was again unloaded there, reloaded aboard small steamers, taken across the Caspian Sea to a Russian port, unloaded, and reloaded on trains that took it finally to the front.

United States Army units handled the cargo work in Bandar Shahpur, and Engineer Corps men were responsible for the piers. It was almost entirely an American operation, and when his ship was ready to leave, Captain Harris applied to the Army for supplies. His chief steward had just informed him that *Arthur P. Davis* was down to her last few days' rations.

The Army supplied the ship with potatoes, flour, coffee, canned milk, some butter, and a large amount of Spam. The Spam came in five-pound tins and in ten-pound tins. It was cooked in every imaginable fashion; the messmen put it on the table fried, stewed, boiled, hashed, mixed with eggs, and just plain. The stuff was doused with mustard, with catsup, with chili sauce, and kept right on tasting like Spam.

Arthur P. Davis left Bandar Shahpur on November 26 and was given orders for Abadan, to take aboard fuel, then was given orders for Durban, South Africa. That long and lonely traverse made, the crew threw overboard with great vehemence all that remained of the Spam. Then she loaded ten thousand tons of coal in Durban and cleared the port for Italy. Her destination was Naples.

The run through the Indian Ocean, the Red Sea, and the Suez Canal was without much incident. But in Port Said the British Naval Control people told Captain Harris that he was to take aboard and ferry across to Naples as deck cargo the guns and trucks of a Polish antiaircraft battery. He was to join a small, six-knot convoy whose only surface protection would come from a British ship equipped with the asdic device. Captain Harris once more considered that luck had turned against him.

The Royal Navy insisted that an antiaircraft balloon should be installed on the Liberty ship's afterdeck. This, when inflated, the British officers said, rose to a height of 1,500 feet, and the steel cable between it and the deck served as deterrent for low-diving German planes; it could very readily slash off a wing tip. Captain Harris objected. He thought that if the balloon had any effect at all, it would be to reduce the speed of the ship because of the drag.

But the British officers talked knowingly of PAC rockets of a similar design that had ripped apart German planes around Malta and over London and on the North Russia run. They spoke of smoke pots that could be opened on the boat deck of a ship and hide her from the enemy and a number of other evasive tactics. Captain Harris could only shrug his shoulders and accept the balloon. Each of them, he realized, cost the United States government $1,500, and was supposed to serve a purpose. There were also in the convoy two small and shaky Greek steamers, both of them coal-burners capable of a maximum speed of six knots. Evasive tactics, for this convoy, would really be a joke.

The convoy sailed from Port Said on January 27, 1944, with the British asdic ship out ahead searching for mines and enemy submarines. Columns were formed and ships took station; the balloons were inflated, their cables unreeled, while overhead the RAF planes from fields outside Cairo kept watch.

The island of Crete was still German-held, though, and as the convoy plugged along westward it came within easy range of the *Luftwaffe*. Down out of the sun at 9:32 on the morning of January 27, the German planes attacked. They were fighter-bombers, and they went for ships at the front of the convoy, hoping to break up its formation and then single out and sink separate ships. Eight ships were hit by bombs, but *Arthur P. Davis* came through safely, and the Nazis did not return. Captain Harris's main concern became his coal cargo; he had been carrying it ever since leaving Durban, and it had a high sulphur content and had been exposed to the fierce heat of the Indian Ocean and the Red Sea.

Captain Harris sneaked out of the convoy and headed at his full speed of better than thirteen knots for the port of Augusta, in Sicily. He reported to the United States Navy authorities there that it was quite possible his ship might at any moment burst into flame from her overheated cargo. He was told to join a convoy, which reached Naples on February 6 after going through a severe storm.

All hands aboard *Arthur P. Davis* felt better when she was ordered the next day to leave the ship-clogged inner harbor and move to an anchorage in the outer bay, where a considerable distance could be maintained between vessels. This was a precaution against enemy bombing attacks; a recent *Luftwaffe* raid upon the port of Bari, on the Adriatic, had caused large damage as bomb-struck ships exploded and took their neighbors with them. But Captain Harris's main concern was the coal. He was afraid his ship would burn up before she blew up.

The chief officer reported to him at 0400 on February 9 that the temperature was 96 degrees in Number Three hold. A blinker message was sent and the shore authorities informed of the ship's condition. The temperature kept on rising; with dawn, wisps of smoke could be seen coming out of the hold.

Captain Harris entered in the log at 9:44 A.M. that the ship was officially on fire. He notified the shore of this, and the signalman broke out the flag hoist that meant "fire aboard." The hoist caused quite a sensation around the anchorage. *Arthur P. Davis* was deep-loaded and gave the appearance of carrying ammunition. The masters of the ships near her wanted to get out fast. They sounded their whistles, sent blinker messages, raised flag hoists, hauled short their anchors, moved just as soon as the engineers could give them steam.

A Navy tug came for *Arthur P. Davis* an hour after she had made her signal. She was towed into a Naples dock which unfortunately was obstructed by a sunken ship. The Liberty tangled with the wreck, but was finally cleared. Her fire hoses were pouring streams of water into the holds while the bilge pumps worked to keep it going out, and the weary fight began.

Nineteen days were needed before the fire was extinguished. The job was interrupted many times by German air attacks, and one night the ship across the dock from *Arthur P. Davis* was struck by a bomb that almost completely wrecked her. It went straight down her stack, through the engine room, through her bottom plates, and then exploded. Commodore Sullivan and his Navy salvage crew were given another difficult piece of work; the vessel had to be patched, pumped out and raised, and cleared from the berth.

Arthur P. Davis already wore a temporary steel patch on the outside of her hull, and this was backed inside the ship by a concrete cofferdam. It repaired the damage done to her bottom when she had been towed into the dock over the submerged ship. The work had been done rapidly by Navy divers and salvage-crew men, but would last, Captain Harris knew, until the Liberty was put in a Stateside shipyard for complete repair.

Sailing light in ballast, *Arthur P. Davis* left Naples on February 28 with no regrets expressed by the crew. She touched at Augusta, Sicily, for orders and was sent across the Mediterranean to Tripoli, in Italian Libya. The cargo assigned her there consisted of German tanks, guns, and half-tracks, all of them perfect examples of *Panzer* equipment captured in the desert fighting. It was wanted by the American Army for inspection and display at home, and Captain Harris loaded it and headed on March 9, 1944, from Tripoli for Algiers, hoping to catch a States-bound convoy.

His luck was good. The Liberty was part of a seventy-ship convoy that left Algiers on March 24 with orders for New York. Most of the ships were riding light, and to avoid rough weather the southern route was taken. But a severe storm met them on April 12 when the convoy was about 350 miles out of New York.

Arthur P. Davis carried some of the German tanks in her Number Two hold. These worked loose from their lashings and started to skate back and forth as the ship rolled deeply in the storm seas. The hold was fifty-seven feet wide. The tanks weighed twenty tons, and the ship's side plates were only three-quarter-inch steel. The chief mate, urgently requested by Captain Harris, went down into the hold to see what might be done. It would not be too long before one of the tanks rammed right through *Arthur P. Davis* and tore a broadside hole that gaped open to the sea.

The mate reported to Captain Harris on the bridge. Then he returned to the hold with the bosun and the best of the sailors. They tossed two-by-four pieces of timber under the treads of the tanks, slowing the big, clanking, khaki-colored monsters down a bit. Next, hawsers were secured around the turrets and the gun muzzles. These were snubbed against sturdy steel upright stanchions in the hold, and after that wire cable was added to the hawsers, and the *Panzer* equipment rested, trapped.

Captain Harris complimented the chief mate; he said the job was well done. The ship returned to her station, and with the rest of the convoy reached New York on April 14 and went to anchor off Staten Island. This was the end of the voyage. Going over to Manhattan from Staten Island the next day, one of the messmen said to a shipmate, "We been goin' around some, you know that?"

chapter 11

THIS was the fourth year of the war and, finally, in May, 1944 the Allies were ready to invade what Hitler called "the Atlantic Wall." The blow was to be struck against Normandy in occupied France. The Germans had sixty divisions deployed along the heavily fortified coast, and Rommel, in command of the defense, had put among them ten of his crack *Panzer* divisions.

The Allies gathered four thousand ships for the assault. The famous English south-coast ports—Southampton, and Plymouth, and Portsmouth—and the Thames River from Gravesend on up to London, and the Bristol Roads, and Liverpool on the Mersey, were filled with ships and cargo. Back from the ports, along the main highways and handy

for truck transportation to dockside, but carefully camouflaged, lay all sorts of invasion material. Allied merchant
marine ships had hauled sixteen million tons of it in less
than a year and also brought to the United Kingdom
aboard transports more than two million troops.

The objective was the Cotentin Peninsula, eighty-two
miles across the Channel from the south coast of England.
It was protected by mine fields and pronged steel "hedgehogs" that lay beneath the surface off the beaches and could
rip the bottom out of a landing craft. Then, up on the
cliffs, were row on row of pillboxes, machine-gun nests, and
concrete bunkers that held powerful cannon. The average
tide flow was twenty feet, and along the Norman coast the
rollers sweeping in from the Atlantic broke incessantly and
always hard.

It was decided at Supreme Headquarters Allied Expeditionary Forces (SHAEF) that an artificial harbor would
have to be built to handle the huge amount of invasion
traffic coming ashore from the vessels to the American
beachhead. Allied specialists in London estimated that
2,000 landing craft would be involved in carrying the
troops, and over them would fly 2,500 gliders loaded with
thousands more. June 4 had been picked as D-day, the
actual date for invasion, but this was delayed until June 6
because of bad weather.

There was every reason for haste. Intelligence reports
told of a secret weapon just produced by Hitler's scientists
and soon to be used—the lumbering, but very effective
"buzz bombs" which appeared over London. But the parts
of the artificial harbor had to be towed into place and then
secured, and the harbor was absolutely essential to the success of the invasion.

BOSTON NEVER LOOKED BETTER. Packed top-
side-bottomside with 1,958 troops, *Aiken Victory*, serving

as a converted transport, warps into her Boston dock July 26, 1945.

Hundreds of tugs, most of them American vessels, stood by to tow the huge caissons across the Channel when the order was given. The caissons were called Phoenixes, the largest sixty feet tall, two hundred feet long, and sixty feet wide. They were equipped with flooding valves so that they could be sunk in place, and on their topsides antiaircraft guns were mounted and manned by soldiers. Each Phoenix was built to give mooring space for seven Liberty ships. Offshore, a series of two-hundred-foot, steel floats would act as a breakwater. Twenty-seven old American and British ships would be scuttled past that to make an additional breakwater. The code name for the artificial harbors was "Mulberry," and Allied headquarters hoped devoutly that the idea was practical. The British were also to build one in their assault area, and nothing like it had ever been tried. Between the floating dock and the shore, pontoon-supported railroad track was to be installed—if the weather was all right.

Convoys formed in a mine-swept area off the Isle of Wight, near Southampton, on the night of June 6 and started the crossing. American merchant marine volunteers made up the crews aboard what were called in code "Gooseberry" vessels, the ships that were to be scuttled off Omaha Beach, one of the points where United States troops were scheduled to land.

Dawn broke gray and chill with plenty of wind. The troop transports that had moved out and taken station during the night off the beaches were exposed to galling German fire. Landing barges as they left the sides of the transports loaded with troops were swept by the famous Nazi 88's that had caused so much damage at Salerno.

Demolition teams, waiting until the last possible moment in order to conceal the attack points from the enemy, were hindered by the high surf and heavily hurt by German fire. Landing barges were sunk or capsized in deep water among the rough steel prongs of the hedgehogs. Men who floundered under the weight of their weapons and equip-ment drowned fast there, while German machine gunners picked off the survivors who were able to swim. But other barges reached the beach, and little groups of men formed and began to answer the Germans and held on during D-day night.

Allied aircraft ranged back and forth above the beaches and bombed the enemy positions and, offshore, British and American warships hammered at the bunkers. But the *Luftwaffe* broke through, strafed the beaches where the men huddled and dropped mines into the sea. An Ameri-can transport, the *Susan B. Anthony*, hit a mine and sank, and a Liberty ship struck another, was badly holed, and was forced to return to England under tow.

Attacks made by the troops on Omaha and Utah beaches took on fierce intensity, and the Germans were driven five miles inland. Sixty miles of coastal fortifications were about to be captured. But supplies were needed, and at dawn a big convoy had come alongshore from Bristol. It carried both troops and cargo. Now was the time for Mulberry, the artificial harbor, to be put into place.

The first of the vessels for the harbor breakwater was hauled into the area at noon. She and her tug were dive-bombed by the *Luftwaffe*, barraged from shore by the 88's, strafed by shrewdly handled machine gunners who picked as targets the men who appeared on deck. Three ships were set in place by sundown, though, their demolition charges exploded in the lower holds, their crews taken off hurriedly aboard the guardian tugs. More were brought in the next day and set against a perversely swinging tide under heavy German fire. They were all old "rust buckets," vessels that had been through severe service on the North Russia run and in the Mediterranean. New Liberty or Victory ships (see Appendix) were much too precious, even for this duty. Still, the volunteer crews felt sad as they jumped down aboard the tugs from the swiftly settling Gooseberry vessels. A ship was a ship, and to sink one was a nasty job; it just added to the score to be paid by the enemy.

The Americans built their Mulberry off Omaha Beach, near the town of Vierville, right inside the six-fathom curve. It had been planned to take a million men during the assault period, and vehicles that weighed sixty tons. Despite German attacks, renewed rough weather and the violent dragging of the tides, it was finished by June 14, and two days later the first LST unloaded at the dock. There had been losses; caissons and tugs had been sunk in German air attacks, and on June 10 the Liberty ship *Charles Morgan* took a bomb through her Number Five hatch.

Charles Morgan had been under air attack for twenty-nine hours straight while she discharged her ammunition cargo. She was about to shove off for England when the German bomb caught her. She was declared a derelict, and all hands abandoned. But her master, Captain William Adams, was reluctant to lose her, and she still floated. He asked for volunteers. His chief officer, R. J. Curtin, and his second officer, R. M. Calder, and Deck Cadet L. B. Wood and eight other men of her crew reboarded. They worked thirty-six hours to get enough water out of her to save her, and during that time they were constantly attacked by the enemy.

It was no good. The ship could not be saved. Captain Adams and his men left her and went aboard the tug that waited alongside. The weather was making up into storm. Omaha Beach offered a poor lee for any ship, and Mulberry was getting pulled apart.

Wind from the northeast rose to thirty knots on the morning of June 19, with seas solid over the breakwater ships. All loading was stopped. Landing craft went out of control. They lurched into the dockside and into the invaluable pontoon roadway to shore. Tugs, launches, barges smashed one another and sank, taking men from their crews with them. That was a night of wild confusion, tragedy, and disaster.

With dawn, Mulberry as a working installation was finished. But the storm lasted for four days. During it, contact with England by sea was completely severed. The American First Army was badly in need of supplies outside Cherbourg. There were over five thousand seriously wounded men to be taken to English hospitals. They waited until June 22, when the storm blew itself out.

The first of the shuttle-run vessels from England came in and anchored in the lee of what was left of the blockship breakwater. The old ships, the bottoms ripped from them by the demolition charges, had kept their stations.

Among them were the Liberty ship *James Iredell* which during her service had been bombed and set afire; and another Liberty, the *Matt W. Ransom*, the target of two direct bomb hits; and the *Exford*, which had run aground at Archangel and been seriously damaged by ice off Iceland. The masters of ten tugs that towed the ships to Mulberry had been decorated by Admiral Sir Bertram H. Ramsey, Allied Naval Commander in Chief, and every officer and man in the volunteer crews had been commended.

Mulberry remained in use at Omaha Beach. The old ships gave a lee to the landing craft as they discharged and loaded. It was all the Americans had as a beachhead base until on June 26 the First Army captured the port of Cherbourg.

The artificial harbor idea had been proven practical despite all of the bad weather. During its period of full operation, Mulberry at Omaha Beach had sent loaded trucks ashore at the rate of almost a hundred within forty minutes. The biggest of the landing craft, the LST's, were discharged in a little over an hour, while the Liberties were steadily unloaded. This was at a time when the First Army had begun to move inland fast and was demanding twenty thousand tons of supplies a day.

Now the course of the war for the American merchant marine swung toward the Pacific. The Allied armies in the last months of 1944 and the first months of 1945 began to crush the Nazis between them. There could be only one end to the European fighting—absolute surrender of the German forces.

But the immense problem of Russian supply still drew cargo ships to Murmansk and Archangel, and there were U-boats on patrol off the North Cape and *Luftwaffe* planes to be called from the Norwegian airstrips. Twelve freighters were sunk in February and March of 1945 with a heavy loss of life.

The Liberty ship *Henry Bacon* was among this lot. She was caught by the Germans when she was homeward-bound and had aboard twenty Norwegian refugees. They were women and children who had escaped to the Soviet Union from the Nazis in their homeland and now were being sent to the United States. Their lives were in great danger when the *Luftwaffe* attacked. The Liberty had become separated from the rest of her convoy in fog off the Lofoten Islands and was running alone. She fought with all she had, but twenty-seven German planes came after her.

The Armed Guard gunners knocked down five planes and exploded four torpedoes with gunfire. Then, though, she was struck in Number Five hold and was mortally hurt. Her people had to get rapidly from her if they wished to live.

But the Germans in their strafing runs had smashed half of the lifeboats. Captain Alfred Carini, the master of the vessel, asked that his senior officers and a number of other crew members stay aboard, giving their lifeboat places to the women and children. This was done. The remaining boats were cleared and pulled safely away from the ship before she pitched her bow high and sank. Captain Carini stood in the bridge wing and waved farewell.

Men who went to sail the Pacific told the story of the *Henry Bacon*. Nothing, they had said, could be worse than the Murmansk run. Out here in the wide, sunny reaches around the coconut islands the war must be much easier. The Murmansk veterans soon found that they were wrong. The Japanese Air Force, fighting with terrible, desperate hatred, was just as formidable as the *Luftwaffe* and perhaps more deadly.

Japanese suicide pilots, half-trained but fully determined to die and take along with them an American ship, had been a serious menace since October 20, 1944, when General MacArthur started his invasion of the Philippines. They came whipping down the sky over Leyte Gulf and dove straight at the American ships which had entered between Dinagat and Homonhon islands. Advance units of the Sixth Army were ashore. There were 650 vessels in the assault fleet, and it seemed as if the landing would be unopposed.

The Japanese who flew the *Kamikaze* planes—*Kamikaze* means "divine wind"—went for the ships that had just been warped alongside the dock at Tacloban. The only warning was the wailing motor screech as the Zeros and Bettys dived.

Armed Guard and merchant gunners were in the gun tubs while the general-alarm bells still sounded, and the guns were quickly hauled around and brought to bear. One of the Liberties was *Adoniram Judson*. She was under the command of Captain Charles A. Jarvis and had been the first to dock. Her gunners were at the pieces for most of the next three days.

The Navy estimated later that *Adoniram Judson* was bombed fifty times during the day of her arrival at Tacloban and eight times that night. She was wracked by a near-miss that left thirty shrapnel holes in her hull. Twelve people aboard her were wounded, seven of them Armed Guard gunners, three crew members, and two Army stevedores. Her score was two *Kamikazes* shot down—one a Zero, the other a Betty—and four probable hits. The crew, working between raids, put her cargo on the dock. A large part of it was steel matting, needed for airstrips where P-38 planes would be put in combat against the Japanese.

Adoniram Judson was given the Gallant Ship award for her share in this action, and Captain Jarvis received the Merchant Marine Distinguished Service Medal.

Another of the Liberties at the Tacloban dock was the *Marcus Daly*. She was fought in the same resolute style by her master, Captain A. W. Opheim, and did a great deal to save the dock from bomb destruction. Her gunners served with steady skill, and were credited by the Navy with three enemy planes. There were two volunteers from the ship's crew among them. They were Alvin Richard Crawford, an able-bodied sailor, and Richard Mattiesen, an ordinary seaman. When a Japanese bomber on a suicide course was shot down, the gunners could not deflect it enough with their fire. It crashed aboard *Marcus Daly* forward in a tangled, flaming mass, and both Crawford and Mattiesen were killed.

General MacArthur sent his personal commendation to the ship. She was made a Gallant Ship. The two volunteers received posthumous Merchant Marine Distinguished Service Medals, and the same decoration went to Captain Opheim. The Armed Guard officer was given the Silver Star, and each of his men the Bronze Star. The *Marcus Daly* was to be remembered for a long time.

The Philippine campaign continued with massive battles at sea in the Surigao and San Bernardino straits. The Japanese Navy was dealt blows from which it could not recover, and the Americans prepared to use Leyte Gulf as a base for a major attack on Luzon. Hundreds of Japanese planes were put into the air in a last attempt to stop ship movements, break the supply lines from the United States.

American merchant ships were supposed to keep out of the forward areas and discharge their cargoes at various Pacific bases—Ulithi, Eniwetok, Manus, and Finschhafen and Hollandia in New Guinea. Theirs was to be the long haul from the American mainland, with the rest to be done by Army and Navy craft. But the need for cargo was too great; the order was ignored or forgotten, and the merchant ships kept right on coming into the Philippines.

Their gunners learned that the *Kamikaze* pilots were more dangerous than ever although in the Philippine fighting more than seven hundred of them had been destroyed. The Japanese pilots flew all kinds of planes, the well-known Zeros and Bettys, and Val and Kate torpedo-bombers, and planes called Jills, and new and heavy types called Zekes and Tojos. The gunners memorized the Japanese plane silhouettes; they described the types to each other, and calculated the rate of fire against the enemy flight speed, which was often as much 450 knots an hour.

Kamikazes roamed the Philippine harbors day and night seeking unprotected ships. One jumped the *Alcoa Pioneer* at San Pedro Bay, in Leyte, setting her afire when the plane smashed squarely into her bridge. She carried cased gasoline in her forward holds, and Captain Andrew W. Gavin, her master, was knocked unconscious and received a broken rib. He got his senses back in time to direct the fire-fighting work which stopped the spread of flame to the gasoline.

A Japanese pilot riddled by bullets and shrapnel, his plane a fiery, whirling wreck, plunged it into Number Two hold aboard the Liberty ship *Juan de Fuca*. This was on December 21 in full daylight during the Mindoro invasion.

The *Kamikaze* bomb exploded in the hold and immediately set the ship afire. Captain C. S. Robbins brought his fire hoses into almost immediate play and saved the ship. But she was one of many to be struck by suicide planes, and most of the vessels, not so lucky, were either burned or were destroyed.

With the Philippines secured, the American advance moved toward Iwo Jima. The little volcanic island was taken after fierce fighting by three Marine divisions, and more than eight hundred ships supported the assault. It was begun on February 19, 1945, and completed on March 17, after casualties that included 4,305 Marine dead.

Merchant marine ships took their part offshore and then at Navy orders began to prepare for the Okinawa operation. The assault was planned for April 1, and would be the greatest ever attempted in the Pacific. The island of Okinawa was in the Ryukyu chain, only 350 miles from the main cities and ports in Japan, and of absolutely vital importance. A garrison force of nearly 200,000 men defended it. The last elements of the Japanese Navy would harass the American fleet, and the *Kamikaze* Attack Corps, filled with recruits, held ten thousand planes ready.

Ships loaded with ammunition, rations, and medical supplies were dispatched across the Pacific by Navy routing officers in the West Coast ports. Their orders were for the big coral atoll of Ulithi in the Caroline group, and for Guadalcanal, and Saipan, and Tacloban. They were to stand by in those assembly areas for the April 1 assault. Tankers that followed them westward carried aviation gasoline and bunker fuel, with P-38's and spare parts lashed on deck. The tankers put into Ford Island overnight, cleared from Hawaii in the morning, and headed for Eniwetok and then Ulithi.

There had never before been anything like this, veteran sailors recognized as they entered the mine-gate at Ulithi. Here within the gray-black walls of coral that broke the force of the long Pacific rollers and left the lagoon calm was an enormous gathering of ships of war. The anchorage contained aircraft carriers, battleships, cruisers, destroyers, destroyer escorts, mine sweepers, and landing craft that mounted rocket batteries.

"Look out, you Jap sons," one sailor said as he studied the scene. "We're coming for you hard this time."

The Okinawa operation called for more than 1,200 ships. These would transport 175,000 soldiers and 88,000 Marines. They sailed on schedule, and the initial landings were made without resistance from the enemy. But the Japanese, not willing to surrender the island, started sudden and savage ground attacks and sent up *Kamikaze* planes from the airstrips.

Three Victory ships, all loaded with ammunition, had been ordered to the Keise Shima anchorage and lay among a number of warships and tankers. When the *Kamikaze* planes came dipping low over the sea in search of targets, it was abruptly decided that the Victories should move. They were sent to a deeply sheltered island offshore and waited there to be discharged.

The *Kamikazes* reached them while their cargoes were still untouched. *Hobbs Victory* managed to blow up a torpedo-bomber before it could reach her. But the next suicide pilot plowed aboard *Logan Victory* and made a fiery shambles of her midships house. The crew could only abandon ship, and later, with a great shower of steel and flame, she blew apart. *Hobbs Victory* went out to sea to get maneuvering room but was caught that same night, April 6, and sunk by a *Kamikaze*. The third ship, *Prairie Victory*, had also moved seaward, and had the luck to remain safe.

While the battle for possession of the island was cruelly fought ashore, another Victory ship full of ammunition arrived on April 27 at the main Okinawa anchorage. She was the *Canada Victory*, and the *Kamikazes* were quick to find her. She was struck in Number Five hold and sunk with the loss of two men, the third mate and a gunner. *Canada Victory* was, though, the last American merchant ship to be destroyed by the enemy in the Pacific.

The Okinawa action was brought to an end on June 14, 1945, and Japanese ability to continue the war was almost finished. The atom bomb was used soon afterward on Hiroshima and Nagasaki, and with that there could only be surrender on the part of Emperor Hirohito. War in Europe had stopped when Hitler committed suicide on May 1, and the Germans sued for peace.

But forty-eight hours before the official date of German surrender on May 6, and with complete knowledge that the vessel he attacked was only a collier, the commander of U-boat *583* sent a torpedo into an American ship named *Black Point*. She was proceeding slowly off Block Island in the Atlantic, and it was very easy for the Germans to sink her.

United States Navy destroyers tracked *U-583* and detonated patterns of depth charges around her. She could not escape them, and with her hull ruptured and her crew drowned, she went down to a bottom depth of fifty fathoms, settled, and stayed there.

Black Point was the last American merchant ship to be lost in the war. Her senseless sinking made clear to many men in the merchant marine how terrible the war had been. Now that it was over, they felt pride of course for what they had done. But, much more, they felt joy in the fact that they could again sail the ships in peace.

APPENDIX

Gallant Ship Awards

The Gallant Ship plaque was designed by the American sculptor Jo Davidson. It was a piece of oak, 3 by 4 feet, on which was mounted a circular bronze disc bearing the silhouette of a merchant ship in a heavy sea. Below the silhouette was the citation itself. The plaque was mounted on the starboard side of the recipient ship at the head of the gangway, if she had survived enemy action.

Each member of a Gallant Ship crew received a ribbon, a dark, sea green in color with sea-gray ends and a silver seahorse symbol superimposed. Each master of a Gallant Ship received the Merchant Marine Distinguished Service Medal.

Nine ships were given the award during World War II. They were the following:

Adoniram Judson, for her part in the Tacloban action, Philippine invasion.

Marcus Daly, for her part in the Tacloban action, Philippine invasion.

Cedar Mills, a T-2 tanker which towed the French warship *Le Triomphant* through a monsoon off the East African coast. *Le Triomphant* had a forty-five degree list, and *Cedar Mills* saved part of her crew from the sea and sharks.

Virginia Dare, for her part in the September, 1942, convoy run to North Russia and subsequent action in the Mediterranean.

Samuel Parker, for action off Tripoli.

Stanvac Calcutta, for action against a German surface raider off Brazil.

Stephen Hopkins, for action against two German surface raiders in the South Atlantic. Ten of her men survived thirty-one days in a lifeboat.

William Moultrie, for her part in the September, 1942, convoy run to North Russia.

Nathaniel Greene, for her part in the September, 1942, convoy run to North Russia and subsequent action in the Mediterranean. The citation issued Captain George A. Vickers, master of *Nathaniel Greene,* follows. It is representative of the language and meaning of all the citations.

UNITED STATES MARITIME COMMISSION
Washington

Office of the Chairman

The President of the United States takes pleasure in conferring the MERCHANT MARINE DISTINGUISHED SERVICE MEDAL on

GEORGE A. VICKERS, MASTER

in accordance with the following
CITATION:
For distinguished service in the line of duty.

In the early spring of 1942, SS NATHANIEL GREENE sailed with a full cargo bound for Russia. Eleven months later, with all housing above deck either demolished or damaged, and with her bow blown away, she was beached by her crew on the North African coast. But in those eleven months she had delivered an urgently needed cargo to our Russian ally; returned to the United Kingdom and repaired and loaded there; and had delivered an equally vital cargo to our own forces in North Africa. On the Russian voyage, the ship survived ten torpedo plane and bomber attacks, was twice attacked by submarines, and had dodged four torpedoes by clever maneuvering. In a sustained attack over three days the ship's guns were credited with the possible destruction of eight enemy planes. On the succeeding voyage, she had discharged nearly all of her military cargo at Algerian ports and was enroute to her final port of call when struck by two torpedoes. In a sinking condition, she was further attacked by enemy aircraft. The planes hit her with three aerial torpedoes but during the fight a shell from one of her guns tore off the tail of one of the attacking planes. With bow underwater; below decks bulkheads ripped out; deck houses wrecked; and steam pipes broken, she was towed in stern first and successfully beached.

Captain Vickers, Master of a gallant ship and a gallant crew, exhibited qualities of leadership and high courage in keeping with the finest traditions of the United States Merchant Marine.

For the President

(Sgd.) EMORY SCOTT LAND

January 8, 1945   Emory Scott Land
Chairman

The United Seamen's Service

The record of the United States merchant marine in World War II would not be complete without the following report. It was shown to the author in March, 1944, when he was with a ship stopping at Glasgow, Scotland. He met the men mentioned in the report. They had just arrived in Glasgow.

They had been brought from the isolated Royal Navy hospital at Loch Ewe, on the bleak western coast of Scotland, 250 miles north of Glasgow. They were the survivors of an American ship, a Liberty bound in convoy for North Russia. The convoy was caught in the worst snow gale to hit Scotland for 150 years, and the ship, burdened by a large deck cargo, became iced over and unmanageable. She fell off station, out of convoy, and piled up on the Scottish coast.

There are other small details which Miss Edith Belle Mainwaring, of the United Seamen's Service, left out of her report. She was forced to go to Loch Ewe by way of Inverness, on the east coast, because of the severity of the storm. The entire north of Scotland was deep in snow. The road was opened for her car by a British Army tank.

The "crofter" folk of whom she writes are the last people in Scotland to wear the kilt as their daily garment and to speak nothing but Gaelic. They brought to the hospital, along with their eggs and honey, bouquets of the famous bluebells of Scotland dug from beneath the snowdrifts. The crofters were barelegged, and some of them barefoot.

When Miss Mainwaring left the Loch Ewe hospital with the survivors and thanked the leader of the crofters, she spoke through an interpreter. The leader said that he and his people were happy that "the Americans" had been saved, and that no thanks need be given.

Her report was made as the regional officer for Scotland of the United Seamen's Service which maintained in Glasgow a former hotel used as a club by American merchant seamen.

March 13, 1944

Memo to: Mr. George Goodfellow, Regional Director, United Kingdom
From: Edith Belle Mainwaring, USS, Glasgow, Scotland

I have recently returned from an intensely interesting trip into the "North Country" where I went to deliver clothing and other necessities to the few survivors of a recent disaster, and to visit other seamen hospitalized in that area. The trip was preceded by a hasty shopping expedition after a long distance consultation as to clothing, sizes, etc. Inquiry as to what was needed brought a message from the men themselves. "Tell the lady if she can imagine us naked

as the day we were born she'll know what to bring."
Through arrangements with the local Army Officers' Store
we were able to purchase woolen underwear, shirts, shoes,
gloves and belts with considerable economy of coupons and
cash. Trousers, jackets, caps and ties were obtained through
a local merchant who is located near the Club and who
often helps us out in times like these; he takes a personal
interest as his own son is in the Merchant Navy. Sweaters
and socks came from a store of these articles recently presented by the Red Cross Field Director who had received a
large shipment of knitted wear for which he had no immediate need. Toilet articles were supplied from our own
emergency shelves.

While alterations to clothing were being made, we set
about securing the necessary passes needed to enter this
zone, which is highly restricted territory. This took a full
day and despite the concentrated efforts of Mr. Gargan and
officials of the Ministry of War Transport, when I finally
left I still lacked the permit essential to get me to my final
destination. However, I was instructed to proceed to my
first stop, some 300 miles distant, and report to a Security
Officer there who might have further advice for me. So,
fortified by several layers of underwear, steamer rug, hot
water bottle, thermos jug and sandwiches, I got under way,
with five large cases of clothing, for the eight-hour trip. The
trains up here have a disconcerting habit of taking one on a
self-conducted tour of Scotland totally unrelated to the
"shortest distance between two points," and this one mean-
dered chuggingly through a snowclad mountainous waste
with the weather growing colder and colder the farther
north we travelled.

On my arrival (in Inverness) I was surprised to be met by Miss Wood, Welfare Officer from one of the hospitals, Mr. Hamilton, representative of the Shipping Commission, and a Security Officer. The latter informed me at once that everything had been arranged for me to continue on my way the following morning—and forthwith disappeared into the night. Mr. Hamilton said a car would be at my disposal for the trip and that he would arrange all the details. Both he and Miss Wood had tried to find accommodations for me in the town, but none were available, and the Superintendent of the Hospital had extended an invitation to make that institution my headquarters. The Hospital is situated some distance in the country so it was well on toward 11 P.M. before we arrived there, but a hot dinner had been prepared for me and I was given a private room in staff quarters where I had the luxury of a bath to thaw me out before turning in. Miss Wood called for me before daybreak and had again arranged to give me a hot meal before leaving.

In the town, Mr. Hamilton met me and said that two of our men had arrived late the previous night to assist in identifying additional bodies which had been found, and that they had worked until morning in preparing them for shipment to Brookwood, where you attended the group burial service for the first men brought in.

With a driver and three men who were joining ships, our car departed at once for the 100-mile trip to the [Loch Ewe] Naval Base. Our route took us over a narrow, tortuous, winding, rutted road encompassed by snow-hooded mountain peaks and ice-enclosed lochs. Except for a few military personnel there was no sign of human life; although occasionally a flock of white-faced sheep or a herd of deer appeared on the mountain side. It was bitterly cold and in such surroundings it was not difficult to imagine how our men had succumbed to suffering and exposure in their fight to escape the icy seas or the rocky cliffs against which their bodies were battered, after the disaster to their ship.

At the military barrier I had a few bad minutes when it was reported that the wires had been down all night and no word had come through which would permit me to enter. After my credentials were studied and the necessity for the pass explained, an attempt was made to phone the Naval Base authorities for confirmation, but these wires were down also. By a curious coincidence, an Intelligence officer entered just then who had been at our Club some months ago in connection with other survivors. Although I had seen him only that once, and he had no advance knowledge of my arrival, he identified me immediately and thus I was permitted to pass.

At the Hospital I was given a cordial welcome by the British Commanding Officer and his staff. This is a small institution where many of our men have been hospitalized and have been shown every consideration, so I was glad to have an opportunity to express our gratitude for these kindnesses.

I found our survivors recovering from shock and although their arms and legs were not yet in good condition, the C.O. felt they would be able to join me the following day and go to Glasgow. The men, most of whom were very young, were as excited as kids over their new clothes. They hobbled about the ward exclaiming over them and exhibiting them to the other patients who seemed very much interested in the whole procedure. Their appreciation was spontaneous and sincere, and it seemed to mean a great deal to them that a USS representative could come in person to see them. When they found they would be permitted to leave the next day, they refused the offer of financial assistance, but asked if they could share their cigarettes and candy with the few British patients remaining in the ward, and seemed to derive intense satisfaction over this privilege.

From them and from a staff member I heard an account of local friendly aid, which I feel should be told here. This story concerns the crofters—the poorest poor of the Scottish Highlands who eke out a barren existence on their tiny bleak farms with a few sheep, a goat or cow, some chickens, and the sparse products of their minute gardens. Their little stone houses—they are scarcely more than huts—appear as occasional dots on the landscape throughout this region. It was the crofters who came to the aid of our merchant seamen on the worst winter's day of the year—a day of snow, hail and biting cold. Over miles of rocky moors they carried jugs of tea, representing weeks of meager rationing, heating it over driftwood fires on the beach, to revive our men exhausted from their battle with the sea, and warm blankets ruined by blood and oil—but what is a blanket more or less when a man is dying, they asked.

For hours they searched the boulder-strewn beach seeking men who, their clothing washed from them, had crawled in their nakedness behind some huge rock to seek shelter. Two survivors are alive today because these people continued their restorative efforts even after officials arriving on the scene had given them up. And, at the hospital, day after day, they have called with a handful of eggs, a tiny jar of precious jam for "the Americans."

INDEX

THE AUTHOR

There are few men as qualified to write of the U.S. Merchant Service as Robert Carse. An experienced seaman, he has spent an equal amount of time on the water as on land during the last forty years, as an able seaman, gunner, master-at-arms, deck watch, and for ten years, chief mate. He not only served with the Merchant Marine in World War II, but was an accredited war correspondent at the same time. Mr. Carse was a member of the ill-fated Murmansk convoy which lost more than half its ships in the 1942 run. He wrote of his experience in his book *There Go*

... ction and
... His novels
... *Go Away*
... a nonfic-
... he Ameri-
... y of Mr.
... hem *The*
... hips, and
... *at Circle*,
... ories and

... l, just off
... ity.